Stencilling
on a Grand Scale

Stencilling
on a Grand Scale

Using Simple Stencils to Create Visual Magic

Sandra Buckingham

FIREFLY BOOKS

BOOKMAKERS PRESS

Second Printing 1998

Cataloguing-in-Publication Data

Buckingham, Sandra, 1944 -
        Stencilling on a grand scale

ISBN 1-55209-143-0

I. Stencil work.   I. Title.

NK8654.B835   1997   745.7'3   C97-930864-X

A FIREFLY BOOK

Published by
Firefly Books Ltd.
3680 Victoria Park Avenue
Willowdale, Ontario
Canada M2H 3K1

Published in the U.S. by
Firefly Books (U.S.) Inc.
P.O. Box 1338, Ellicott Station
Buffalo, New York 14205

Produced by
Bookmakers Press Inc.
12 Pine Street
Kingston, Ontario K7K 1W1
613-549-4347
tcread@sympatico.ca

Design by
Linda J. Menyes
Q Kumquat Designs

Color separations by
Friesens
Altona, Manitoba

Cover color separation by
Mutual/Hadwen Inc.
Ottawa, Ontario

Printed and bound in Canada by
Friesens
Altona, Manitoba

Printed on acid-free paper

Acknowledgments

I've lost count of how often, during the past six months, my kids have interrupted my painting to ask, "When's supper, Mom? We're hungry." Totally preoccupied with my own work, I'd look up at them, unaware of time, family or even whether there was any food in the house, thinking only that every day, I was slipping a little further behind schedule. This book turned out to be far more demanding of time, effort and space than I had thought it would be at the outset. I could not have finished it without the help and support of many people.

I would like to thank my immediate family for putting up with the constant mess and the expanding domain of my work, as I took over one room after another in our house, storing panels and doors wherever I wasn't painting. Thanks to my husband, Carl Walters, for putting food on the table whenever I couldn't and for taking up the slack on the domestic scene. Thanks to my sister, Linda Buckingham, for her support, ideas and invaluable feedback, as well as for stencilling several large projects for the book and helping during the photo shoot. She lifted my spirits whenever I felt discouraged or overwhelmed and kept me going. My niece, Dana Savage, painted walls and ceilings for me on her days off work and helped feed a hungry crew. My mother, Pat Shore, helped keep me focused. "My" carpenter, Stephen Davies, did a wonderful job of inventing and building a giant easel and collapsible set, as well as helping me move stuff around and giving me advice on stress management. Thank you, Georgina King, for the beautifully laundered and ironed denim overalls. Both Jane Rainford of Country Furniture and Karen Gruninger Shu of Peasantries once again gave me free rein to borrow literally anything from their delectable stores for photo props. Thanks to our photographers, Clinton Hussey and assistant Mark Gilbert in Vancouver and Preston Schiedel in Kingston, Ontario, who managed to stay creative and patient throughout long hours under sometimes difficult conditions. The Vancouver and Kingston photo shoots would have been impossible without the generous help and gofering of Shirley and John Menyes. Long-distance thank you to Robert Brideau for his unseen but much appreciated help behind the scenes. Tracy Read of Bookmakers Press got this project off the ground, and she and Susan Dickinson managed to keep cool and forgo official holidays long enough to do a great job of editing. Thank goodness for fax and E-mail!

Finally, this book would not have been possible without the design work, creative suggestions and support of Linda Menyes, who worked with me from start to finish and to whom this book is dedicated. This is the third book that Linda and I have produced, and for each of them, she has been more of a collaborator than just a designer or an editor. She even learned to stencil! Normally, she gets two words of credit in small type on the copyright page ("Designed by…"), while my name goes on the cover. This time, I would like to give her recognition for her contributions above and beyond the call of duty. Thank you, Linda. I couldn't have done it without you!

To Linda J. Menyes
(1961-1997),
book designer, friend
and kindred spirit

Contents

◇

Introduction 9

Technical Review 13

Freeform Stencilling 35

Starting Small 45

Focus on Flowers 57

Basic Structures 69

Setting Limits 83

Floors 111

Stone & Shadow 123

Frankly Fake 139

Sources 146

Index 148

Introduction

◇

*"One can never consent to creep
when one feels an impulse to soar."*
—*Helen Keller,* The Story of My Life

◇

The Creative Itch

The Creative Itch

While our public personas are typically defined by our work, most of us plug away at our jobs simply to put food on the table. What we *are* may have very little to do with how we earn a living. Often, we're just waiting for the weekend, when our passions can feed our souls.

Peel away the workaday veneer of that "average" neighbor down the street, and you may be surprised at what you find: a supermarket clerk who forges iron in her spare time; an oceanographer who plays the bagpipes; a psychologist who wing-walks; a teacher who grows bananas on Canada's West Coast.

Somehow, the word "hobby" belittles the creative force that motivates and inspires, that gives us a reason to get up in the morning. We don't know where it comes from, only that it is diverse and compelling. For one of my sons, it's carving a slow turn in the air, searching out the currents that will lift the long wings of his glider and let him soar higher, farther. For my other son, it's playing alchemist with flavors, smelling, tasting and mixing garden herbs or exotic spices, manipulating the aromas wafting from the cookpot. For my husband, it's making the perfect cast, watching the gossamer line glint in the sun as it drops the fly softly on the dappled surface of a deep-river pool.

For me, it's messing with paint.

I have no formal training in art. I just happen to love color and pattern, and I can't help playing with them. Paint is a friendly and inexpensive medium for this, and stencils are the simple tools that let me use paint in an infinite variety of ways.

You don't have to paint for a living to use this book, and you don't have to have artistic talent. Stencils can take care of the talent part. What you *do* need is the creative itch to make painted images and the desire to produce something more exciting than repeatable borders. This book shows you how to use simple stencils in non-conventional ways, with results that are far grander than the stencils would suggest. It starts by teaching you a few basic techniques that can be used to make something simple, such as your annual greeting cards. Then it works those techniques into projects that increase in size and complexity with each chapter.

Many of these projects are full-scale murals, yet with few exceptions, they are produced with small one- or two-piece stencils. Here, modest templates are used repeatedly to build big images. Overlapping prints and layered colors make the images look complex. Transparent shading makes them look real. There are no tricks, and there's no big expense. It's just a matter of patience, of working in sections and layers, and *that* makes it seem like magic.

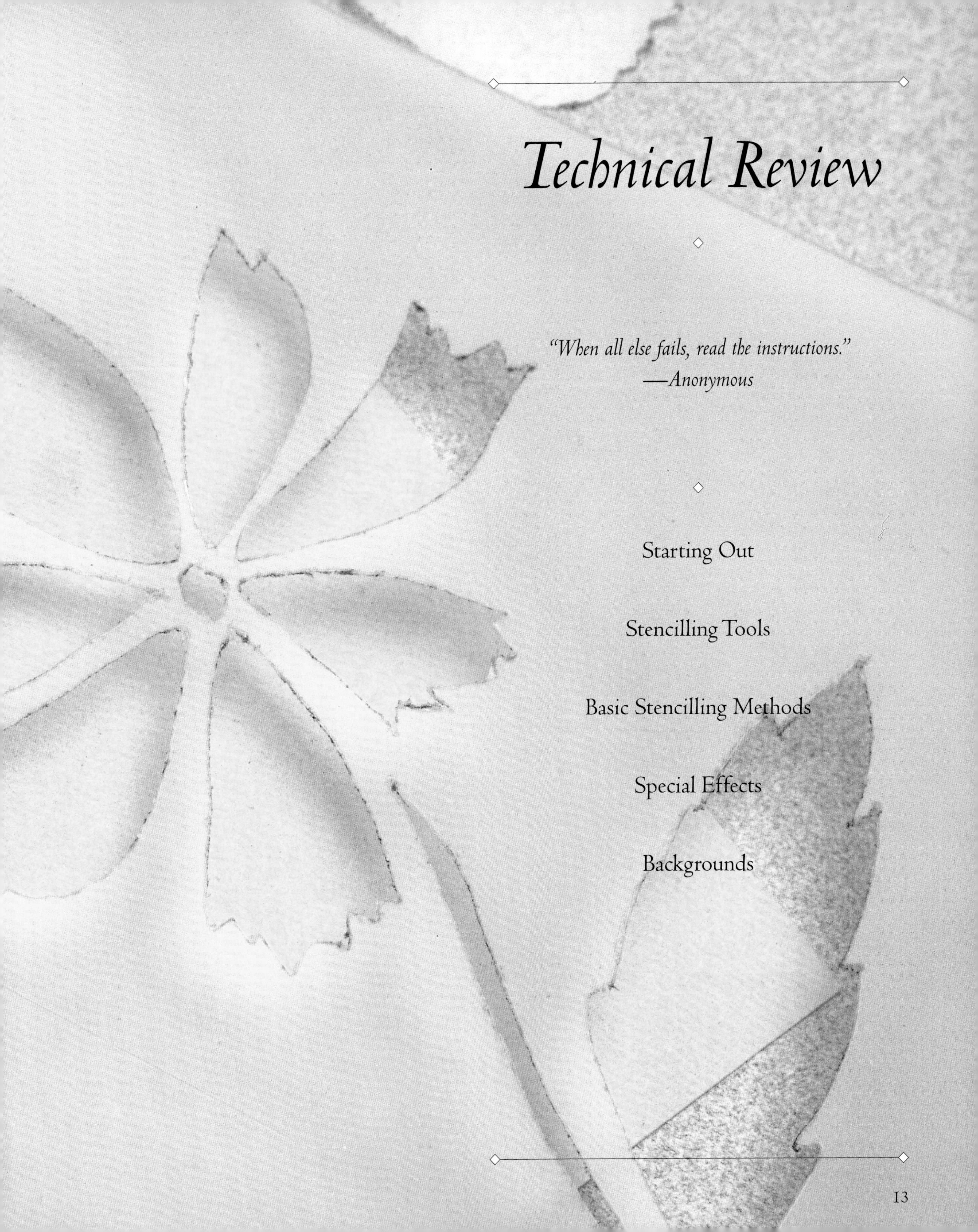

Technical Review

"When all else fails, read the instructions."
—Anonymous

Starting Out

Stencilling Tools

Basic Stencilling Methods

Special Effects

Backgrounds

Stencils

As the only woman enrolled in the fourth-year physics program at my university back in the 1960s, I went to class every day convinced that everyone was waiting for me to screw up. Whether I was building diodes or measuring the speed of light, my overriding goal was therefore pretty basic: I wanted to avoid making any monumental blunders. This was a significant challenge for me, because I was part of a generation of women who had reached adulthood without ever having so much as looked at an electrical circuit or peeked under the hood of a car. That set me apart from my classmates, who had probably found voltmeters and wire-strippers under the Christmas tree by the time they'd turned 6.

Facing the daily prospect of public humiliation, I developed a habit that saved me a lot of grief: I read the instructions. In fact, I was obsessed with instructions. That was my salvation (though it now puts me at odds with my husband every time we acquire a new electronic device). In those days, the guys simply waltzed into the lab and started flipping switches. If something didn't work, they flipped a few more switches. On, off, on, off. As a last resort, they might, furtively, consult the manual. I was the only student that year who didn't have to disassemble and clean the backed-up vacuum diffusion pump, because I was the only one in the class who'd read the instructions before turning it on.

Of course, if you're using the same piece of equipment every day, you won't still be reading the manual 10 years later. At that point, you're more likely to have modified the method and built your own version of the apparatus. In creative fields, this happens quickly. You may begin by copying something, but almost before the brush touches the paper, you are already envisioning a dozen other ways to paint an apple.

I don't expect many of you will be doggedly following every step of the methods you find here once you've done half a dozen murals or freeform projects. You cannot help finding ways that work better or more comfortably for you, just as I'm sure I, too, will be doing some things differently before this ink is dry. But what I've presented here is a good place to start. Following these instructions will guide you beyond the scope of ordinary stencilling while helping you to avoid the many learning mistakes I made. Once you are comfortable with the basics, well—as I've said before—whatever works is the right way to do it.

I expect that most people reading this book will have already tried their hand at some form of stencilling; those stencilling enthusiasts can skip the review of basic tools and techniques and probably not miss much. For the complete novice, however, the first chapter provides enough information to get started. Once you are able to make a good, clean stencil print, you are ready to take the next step.

Hand-Cut Frosted Mylar Stencil

The simplest stencils have an entire design cut into a single template. The gaps between the cutouts, called bridges or ties, help define the details of the design (i.e., they separate one petal of a flower from the next). So-called bridgeless stencils use extra templates, or overlays, to fill in the gaps. They allow for more realistic designs, with, for example, distinct petals touching or overlapping each other.

◆ **Commercial Stencils**
The best commercial stencils are made of transparent Mylar, either clear, tinted or frosted, and are cut by laser, die or drill.
◇ *Die-Cut Stencils*
Die cutting is the oldest method of manufacture. Stencils that include multiple overlays are usually printed with overlay outlines to help you line them up correctly.
◇ *Laser-Cut Stencils*
Lasers make the smoothest cuts and are the tool of choice for most of the high-end stencil companies. The computer-controlled cutting path of drills and lasers can form just about any shape. Laser-cut stencils use a "point registration" system that is highly accurate. Small diamonds, triangles or circles are cut into the corners of each overlay and matched up for proper positioning.
◇ *Tin and Brass Stencils*
You can also find commercial stencils made from tin or brass. Most of these are very small, designed for craft use only.
◆ **Homemade Stencils**
Homemade stencils can be made from a variety of materials, either transparent (Mylar, acetate, vinyl, overhead-projection film) or opaque (stencil card, freezer paper).
◇ *Mylar*
Mylar is the strongest stencil

material. It comes in several thicknesses: 5-mil is pretty standard for homemade stencils. Any thicker is too hard to cut; any thinner is a bit flimsy. But that's just a guideline. Use whatever you feel comfortable with.
◇ *Freezer Paper*
Freezer paper also makes excellent, very inexpensive stencils, even though it is opaque. Freezer paper is coated on one side with a thin plastic film; the plastic side is the side on which you apply the paint. It's so easy to cut that I usually cut three or four at the same time by stacking several sheets, using spray glue to keep them from slipping. These stencils are surprisingly durable; you need the extras only to replace ones with too much paint buildup (you can't wash them). Paper stencils are handy for rounding the corners of a room because you can easily fold them right into the corners. When using a Mylar stencil, I find it handy to make a few freezer-paper copies, just for using in the corners.
◇ *Stencil Card*
Stencil card is an old-fashioned material, a card stock treated so that it is impervious to paint. It is difficult to cut but, because it is so stiff, is very useful for really large stencils. Try manhandling a four-foot-tall Mylar stencil some day, and you will appreciate the virtues of stencil card.
◇ *Acetate and Vinyl*
Acetate and vinyl are less satisfactory materials. Acetate tears easily, and vinyl is floppy, especially in warm weather. But, in a pinch, they work quite adequately. In a real pinch, you can make a lot of things work adequately—vinyl tablecloths, cardboard file folders, cereal boxes.

Laser-Cut Blue Mylar Commercial Stencil

Hand-Cut Clear Mylar Stencil

Hand-Cut Freezer-Paper Stencil

Die-Cut Commercial Stencil

Hand-Cut Stencil-Card Stencil

Brass Commercial Stencil

12

13

Paint

◆ Acrylic and Latex Paints

For environmental reasons, acrylic and latex paints have become the standard media for most craft and home-decorating uses. They are fast-drying, inexpensive, odorless and available everywhere in hundreds of colors. Some latex paints are sold in very small containers, just enough to let you test a color before ordering a gallon. This is perfect for stencilling—you can choose exactly the colors you want without spending a lot and without accumulating cans of leftovers. My own brand of acrylic latex for roller stencilling comes in small, economical squeeze bottles for easy dispensing.

Acrylic and latex paints can be applied with a stencil brush, a sponge or a foam roller. Light colors tend to be opaque, and darker colors more transparent. Transparency, drying time and blending qualities can all be manipulated by adding different proportions of extender or acrylic glaze to the paint. Mixed with a bit of glaze (such as Buckingham Blending Glaze), acrylic and latex paints can be made to blend just as smoothly as the solid paints described below, yet they still dry fast enough to make them safe to use with multiple overlays.

Acrylic craft paints normally dry particularly fast and hard under stencilling conditions, making them difficult to use with rollers. Adding a glaze or an extender makes them much easier to stencil with.

◆ Solid Stencil Paints

Solid stencil paints have been around for a long time in the form of sticks and crayons. With an oil-based formula (but soap-and-water cleanup), solid paints dry slowly, which makes them blend very well. It also means that they smudge easily, making them tricky to use with multiple overlays. It's easy to make these paints look airbrushed and transparent but difficult to build up a dense layer of color. Beginners like solid paints because they don't bleed under a stencil (but with proper technique, neither do liquid paints).

◆ Fabric Paints

Fabric paints can be used to stencil cloth, paper and sometimes, depending on the brand, solid surfaces. While acrylics and solids can also be used on cloth, they dry stiff. Wherever softness is essential—on baby clothes or boxer shorts, for example—you should use real fabric paints. They usually require some sort of heat treatment to make them washable.

◆ Glaze, Extender

With the development of acrylic formulas, glazes and extenders have become mainstream paint sundry products for the do-it-yourself market. They are sold in paint, hardware and craft stores.

An extender is a paint additive that slows drying time. If you add a lot, it will also make the paint less opaque. This is a very useful product if you stencil in a hot climate.

A glaze is a transparent medium that you can tint with paint or universal colorants. It is used to create transparent layers of color, whether in faux finishes or stencilling. Glazes also dry more slowly than paint, but the open, or working, time varies from brand to brand. Open time also decreases when you add paint to the glaze.

◆ Shadow Glaze

When I use the term *shadow glaze* in this book, I mean an acrylic glaze tinted with raw umber colorant. You can mix your own or use a pre-tinted brand such as Symphony Faux & Decorative Glaze (in raw umber). For some strongly colored projects, you may need a deeper shadow medium or one with a hint of another hue. In this case, you can blend a little paint or colorant into your basic shadow glaze.

◆ Other Paints

Special effects can be achieved by stencilling with metallic paints, interference paints or clear acrylic varnish. Some stencillers prefer to use canned spray paints. Personally, I find spray painting too messy and smelly. You must wear a mask, and you need to spend a lot of time carefully masking anything you don't want painted. Just in case you want to try it, I have included in the Sources, at the back of the book, references to books that discuss spray stencilling.

Any decorated surfaces that are subject to wear and tear should be protected with several coats of acrylic varnish. This means floors, doors and most furniture. However, I rarely varnish walls. My stencil paint is as tough as any wall paint.

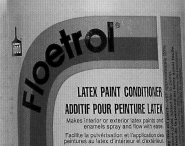
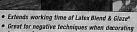

Stencilling Tools

Applicators

◆ Stencil Brushes

The traditional tool for stencilling is a stencil brush. It has densely packed bristles bound and trimmed into a roughly cylindrical shape, rather like an old-fashioned blunt-cut shaving brush. Bristles can be stiff or supple; the best choice depends on how you apply the paint—i.e., stiff for pouncing, soft for rubbing or swirling, very soft for blending. Handles come in a variety of shapes; some are easier for pouncing, others for rubbing.

◆ Foam Rollers

For speed, nothing beats a high-density foam roller used with acrylic or latex paint. You can minimize lap lines by choosing a roller with rounded ends and adding some glaze or extender to the paint. Broad shading (random or controlled) and color blending are easy with a roller. Detailed shading and color manipulation can be done with a stencil brush after laying down most of the color with a roller.

◆ Sponges

Sponges (cellulose or sea) produce stencilled prints with a mottled coloring, useful for stencilling stone urns or balustrades. Fine-textured makeup sponges can be used for softly shading small stencils.

◆ Airbrushes

Professional graphic artists have long used airbrushes for stencilling, but these are rather expensive and technical for widespread common use. You can, however, put thinned paint in a spray mister for coarse-grained spattering through a stencil, which is useful for adding texture to stencilled "stone," for instance.

Foam Rollers and Handle

Various Stencil Brushes

Makeup Sponges

Cellulose Sponge

Sea Sponge

Various Stencil Brushes

19

Stencilling Tools

Miscellaneous Equipment

▷ Palette trays, especially ones with a slightly raised edge, are indispensable for mixing paint colors and working paint into brushes or rollers. Cookie sheets covered with freezer paper make a good substitute, albeit somewhat inconvenient if someone wants to bake when you are in full painting mode.

▷ A putty knife or palette knife is used for roller stencilling (to spread a thin layer of paint on the palette), as well as for mixing colors.

▷ Artist's brushes of various sizes and shapes are handy for adding freehand accents to your stencilling.

▷ You'll need lots of paper towels to remove excess paint from brushes or rollers.

▷ If you cut your own stencils, you'll need an X-acto knife, spare blades, a cutting mat and stencil material (i.e., Mylar sheets or freezer paper). For cutting heavy Mylar, a heat cutter is easier to use than a knife. This tool, shaped like a very fine soldering iron, is also useful for cutting lines that are ragged or highly irregular in shape.

▷ Low-tack stencil adhesive and painters' tape are needed to hold stencils in position. The adhesive is available as a spray or solid stick, but most people find that the spray is by far the easiest to use. Spray adhesive is used to keep fine bridges on the stencil from shifting while you apply the paint. It also provides enough stick to keep lightweight stencils on a wall.

▷ Low-tack painters' tape is invaluable. Use it to hold up heavier stencils, to make stripes, to mask parts of your work and to make removable registration marks.

▷ Small plastic squeeze bottles with very fine tips are useful for outlining stencilled images, for adding veins and stamens or even for writing lines of poetry alongside your ivy.

▷ Small plastic misting bottles filled with water are great for preventing paints and rollers from drying out. Hold the bottle above your palette, and pump it a few times to spread a fine mist of water over the paint.

▷ Clean, empty shampoo bottles, the squeezable kind, make handy containers for storing latex paint because they let you shake the paint and neatly dispense the small dollops used in stencilling. It's an easy way to eliminate the mess of stirring a big can and scooping out dripping spoonfuls. Just make sure you label the bottles, or you might end up trying to shampoo with latex paint, as I once did. Use a funnel to fill the bottles. (Keep such bottles away from children and absent-minded spouses.)

▷ Watercolor pencils are useful for creating shadowed crevices and very fine marble veins.

▷ Once you start stencilling with many different layers of images, you'll find liquid frisket, or masking fluid, a very useful addition to your supplies. Look for the special frisket applicator shown in the photograph, which makes applying this liquid latex so much easier than using a brush.

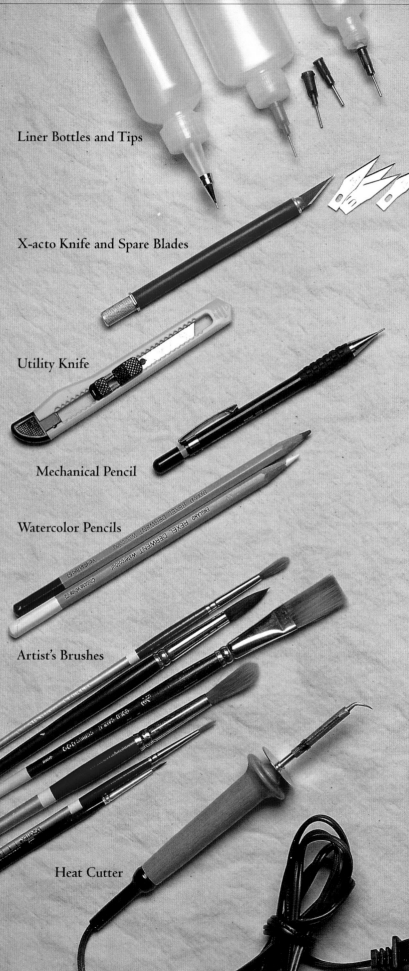

Liner Bottles and Tips

X-acto Knife and Spare Blades

Utility Knife

Mechanical Pencil

Watercolor Pencils

Artist's Brushes

Heat Cutter

Empty Squeezable
Shampoo Bottles

Putty Knife

Paper Towels

Funnel

Palette Knife

Palette Tray

Low-Tack
Painters' Tape

Liquid Frisket
and Applicator

Stencil Adhesive Spray

Misting Bottles

Ruler

Cutting Mat

Basic Stencilling Methods

Stencil Cutting

◆ With a Knife

◇ *Opaque Stencils*

▷ Spray the back of your paper pattern with stencil adhesive. Place pattern on top of stencil material, smoothing it down so that it adheres evenly.

▷ To protect your tabletop, place your work on a cutting board or on several sheets of smooth cardboard.

▷ With a sharp blade, cut along the lines of the pattern, cutting through both pattern and stencil material (1). Keep turning the stencil so that you are cutting toward yourself and finishing smooth curves without lifting the blade.

▷ Remove pattern (2).

◇ *Transparent stencils*

▷ Spray the underside of your Mylar with a light coat of stencil adhesive. Place Mylar sheet, glue side down, on top of your paper pattern, and place a cutting board under the pattern (3).

▷ Following the pattern lines visible through the Mylar, cut through the Mylar (4). It's all right if the pattern gets cut. If you need to keep it intact (for another overlay), simply tape the cuts on the reverse side of the pattern before peeling the stencil and pattern apart.

▷ Remove pattern.

◆ With a Heat Cutter

A slightly less accurate but physically easier method of cutting Mylar stencils involves using a heat cutter instead of an X-acto knife. A heat cutter looks like a fine soldering iron. It's more expensive than a knife, so before buying it, try one out if possible. You follow the same steps as for transparent stencils, except that you work on a sheet of smooth cardboard, poster board or glass instead of a cutting board (1, 2).

A heat cutter is very useful for designs with lots of irregular wiggles (which are hard to cut with a knife) and for thick Mylar stencils (which quickly wear out fingers and blades when cut with a knife).

Hard-Surface Stencilling

The next two sections illustrate the basic techniques common to most stencilling projects.

A few steps are the same whatever the method. First, you need to hold the stencil in place—most people use stencil adhesive or painters' tape or both. After making a print, you lift the stencil, move it to its next position and press it into place. The tack of the adhesive or tape should last for many prints without having to be replaced.

If used too enthusiastically, stencil adhesive can leave a slight residue on the stencilled surface. It's best to spray it sparingly on the underside of the stencil (do this outdoors so that you don't inhale any or get it on your floor) and to give it a few minutes to dry before using the stencil. If it is too sticky, blot the stencil on a textile before using.

Remember that the primary function of spray glue is to keep wobbly parts of the stencil still, although it will also hold lighter stencils on the wall. Use painters' tape to support bigger stencils. It has more holding power than the stencil glue does but is not tacky enough to lift paint (as masking tape often does).

The key to good stencilling, no matter what the method or what the paint, is to use an absolute minimum of paint. You work enough paint onto your applicator to get it evenly coated, then you remove most of it with paper towels so that the applicator (brush or roller) is almost dry before it touches the stencil. It is this "dry brush" approach that will give you a nice, clean print with no paint bleeding under the edge of the stencil. Spray glue does not prevent bleeding—it only holds the stencil in place. If you have bleeding, there is only one thing wrong: too much paint on your applicator.

Basic Stencilling Methods

Hard-Surface Stencilling

◆ **Using a Stencil Brush With Acrylic or Latex Paint**

Acrylic paint has been a stencilling standby for decades, but you can use it interchangeably with latex house paint. The main advantage of both paints is also their main disadvantage—they dry very fast, especially with the very thin coatings used in stencilling. This is a good thing in that it prevents smudging and allows you to use overlays in rapid succession. But fast-drying paint doesn't blend smoothly on your work. It also hardens quickly on the brush, leaving the bristles stiffly caked with dried paint.

You can solve both problems by adding a small amount of clear glaze or extender to the paint before starting. The more glaze you add, the more transparent the paint becomes and the more slowly the paint dries, so you should experiment a little before you start a project.

Another approach is to prime your brush with some glaze, then dab it into paint (instead of premixing); touch it to the glaze again whenever the brush starts getting stiff. When I get really caught up in my work, I mix colors right on my brush, dabbing it into one color, then another, then into some glaze. I swirl the brush around on the palette to more or less mix everything, then rub off the excess on paper towels.

To stencil with a brush and a water-based paint, follow these steps:

▷ Pour a small amount of paint onto a palette or plate.

▷ Your stencil brush must be dry to start with. Work a tiny amount of glaze into the bristles, then dab them into the paint puddle (1) so that you pick up a small amount of paint on the ends of the bristles (see note above about glaze).

▷ Without adding more paint, rub the brush around in circles on the palette so that the paint is evenly distributed over the ends of the bristles.

▷ Rub the brush around in circles on some paper towels to remove most of the paint (2).

▷ Holding the brush straight up and down, apply paint through the stencil cutouts (3) either by pouncing the brush up and down (also known as stippling) or by rubbing the brush around in circles (swirling). Build up the color slowly—the key to good stencilling is to add paint gradually. If your brush starts taking off more paint than it is adding, stop and let the image dry thoroughly before continuing.

▷ The finished print almost always looks darker once the stencil is removed, so before you add too much paint, lift a corner of the stencil from time to time to check on your progress.

▷ Some people shade stencil prints by building up stronger color around the edges.

▷ You can also add other colors through the same stencil, blending them or not, for an image with broken color. Most people use a separate brush for each color. If you rinse out a brush, it must dry completely before reuse.

▷ The paint on your brush will dry quite quickly, so every once in a while, you should tap the brush on a damp sponge or work a little glaze into the bristles. This makes the paint workable again without getting the bristles too wet.

◆ Using a Stencil Brush With Solid Stencil Paint

When not in use, solid stencil paints form a skin on the surface. You need to peel this off before you can use the paint (1). Depending on how fastidious you are about not getting paint under your nails, you can use your thumb, a paper towel, masking tape or a blunt knife to scrape off this skin. Then follow these steps:

▷ Rub a dry stencil brush in circles over the exposed surface in the jar to pick up paint (2). It should feel rather creamy.

▷ Rub the brush in circles on your palette to make sure the paint is evenly distributed on the brush. Nothing spoils a print faster than a glob of paint hiding in the bristles.

▷ Rub the brush in circles on a paper towel to remove any excess (3).

▷ Rub or stipple paint over the stencil (4), building up color gradually and shading if desired. Because of the long open time, this paint blends and shades very easily. It is easy to obtain an airbrushed effect and to blend in other colors.

▷ You can mix solid colors by rubbing your brush into one pot of color, then another, and working the brush around on your palette to mix them.

▷ To get very dark or rich coloring, you will have to work in stages, because this paint is rather transparent. Let your first pass dry overnight, then restencil it to add more color.

▷ Remove the stencil carefully. The paint will smudge very easily (5) until it has dried for a few hours.

Basic Stencilling Methods

Hard-Surface Stencilling

**◆Roller Stencilling
With Latex or Acrylic Paint**
This is a relatively new technique—fast, easy and ideal for large projects. If you are using latex house paint, transfer some to a plastic squirt bottle (empty shampoo bottles work well) for ease of dispensing the small amounts needed. Adding a little extender or glaze to these paints (especially to acrylic, which dries particularly hard and fast) makes them easier to work with (but it also makes them more transparent).

This method will not work with nap rollers—they hold too much paint. You need a high-density foam roller, with rounded edges if possible, and a palette tray—something flat with shallow edges to keep the paint from running off. Start with a dry roller.

▷ Pour a small puddle of paint at one end of the tray. Use a spatula to spread the paint out in a long, thin layer (1).
▷ Run the foam roller through this layer of paint, covering the whole surface of the roller. Then, without adding more paint, work the roller back and forth until the paint is worked evenly into the foam (2).
▷ Remove all excess paint from the roller by rolling it back and forth on a pile of paper towels (3). At this point, check the paint left on the towels. If you see stripes of dense paint interspersed with

fainter bands of paint, the paint is unevenly loaded. To correct this problem, repeat the previous step, if necessary overloading the roller with paint. Then remove all the excess. You should be able to drag the roller lightly over a surface and leave just a light, even trace.
▷ Work the roller over the whole surface of the stencil (4), pressing lightly at first and increasing the pressure only as the print gets fainter. Check the print before adding more paint. Build up the color gradually by going over it again, adding emphasis to any area you want shaded. Usually, you can get very effective "self-shading" just from the random variations of the roller. To keep the roller from drying out, run it lightly over a damp sponge periodically. Put it in a sandwich bag when you take a break.
▷ If paint bleeds under the stencil, either you have too much paint on the roller or you are pressing too hard (5, left). If your print is really uneven, then the paint has not been loaded evenly on the roller (5, right).

Stencilling on Canvas

◆ Primed Canvas

Stencilling large pieces of canvas (too big to be washed and preshrunk) for use as wall hangings or floorcloths is a little different from doing a T-shirt. It's more like working with a flimsy section of wall that tends to shrink wherever you apply paint. The best way to deal with this is to prime the whole piece with a generous coat of gesso or flat latex paint (2) after stretching and stapling the canvas out on a frame, a piece of plywood or a section of basement wall (1). Use strong staples, and place them no more than a few inches apart, because the whole canvas will try to shrink as the primer dries, and the force of this shrinking is quite strong. If this sounds like too much work, you can always buy the canvas preprimed at an art-supply store.

Once the primer has dried, you can move the canvas, if you wish, before stencilling, but sometimes it's more convenient just to leave it where it is, especially if you want to add color or a faux treatment to the background. After you do remove the canvas, trim off the stapled edges using a sharp utility knife and a metal-edged ruler.

Stencilling on primed canvas is more like working on a wall than on fabric, because you are putting paint on a surface that is already painted. Acrylic and latex paint work well, as do some fabric paints. A few fabric paints do not adhere well to painted surfaces, so test them before using.

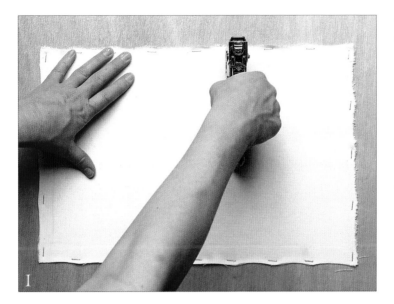

◆ Unprimed Canvas

Stencilling a large, unprimed canvas is a little tricky, because selective shrinking at the sites of your motifs may cause the whole surface to buckle. You can minimize this by stretching out the canvas and stapling it to a frame or work surface, just as you would if you were going to prime it.

Basic Stencilling Methods

Overlays and Registration

◆Single Stencil

The best way to explain the use of overlays is to start with an image that uses a single stencil only and show what additional overlays can mean in terms of color and design.

This first stencil of a flower, stem and leaf is cut as a single stencil. The simplest approach is to stencil the whole thing with a single color (1, 2). By using small brushes, it is also quite easy to color the flower yellow, for instance, and the foliage green (3). Some of the green will end up on the flower and some of the yellow on the leaves, because the brushes can't help straddling the bridges between the two. This inter-mingling of colors is termed broken color. Stencillers often exaggerate the effect, deliber-ately expanding the areas of overlap and adding other colors as well, because this technique produces a more in-teresting print from a single simple stencil.

◆Color Separation

If you want to be really fussy about which colors go where, either mask off parts of your stencil or separate the colors by putting all the cutouts belong-ing to one color on their own stencil sheet. These separated stencils are called overlays. The tricky part is placing the second overlay in the right position, or registering it, so that all the parts go where they are supposed to. For most laser-cut stencils, registration is done by lining up tiny cutouts in the shape of triangles, circles or diamonds.

Using the previous design as an example, the first overlay might print the flower (1, 2). Before removing the stencil, trace the registration triangles with a fine pencil (I use a 0.5 mm mechanical pencil). So as not to mark the sten-cilled surface, I place a small piece of low-tack tape under each registration triangle beforehand (1).

Line up the triangular cut-outs on the second overlay with the traced triangles (3). Now the stencil is in perfect position to be painted (3, 4).

28

◆No Bridges

To make this flower look more realistic, we must eliminate the bridges on the print so that the petals can touch each other, even overlap. To do this, we put adjacent petals on separate overlays.

In this example, the first stencil prints roughly half the petals (1, 2). Note the registration marks.

The second overlay is positioned with the help of the registration triangles (3) and printed, to complete the flower head (4). By using a light touch on the second overlay, you can allow the overlap to show through if you wish, making the petals look translucent.

Use a third overlay to complete, adding stem and leaves (5, 6).

1

3

5

2

4

6

Special Effects

Shading

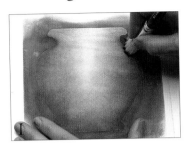

Stencilled images can be given a three-dimensional feeling by appropriate shading. For example, a vase can be made to look round by applying slightly darker paint to the side and bottom edges (1, 2). Additional structure, in the way of ridges and crevices, can be added simply by running a brush with darker or lighter color along the edge of a piece of painters' tape (3, 4) or along a straight edge of Mylar. Highlights can also be added freehand.

Shadows

Shadows add the final touch of realism to stencilled trompe l'oeil. You can shadow vines and branches easily by shifting the stencil slightly in the direction you want the shadow to be cast (1). Stencil the exposed gap lightly with shadow glaze (tinted if you wish a different hue), tapering off where the stencil overlaps the painted leaves. The transparent color will hardly show up on the leaves (2), so you don't have to be too fastidious in your tapering.

Freehand painted vine shadows are also very effective. Use a round artist's brush or a liner brush loaded with a blend of shadow glaze and water. Work quickly and loosely to trail a faint echo of the vine shape (3). Make the vine seem closer or farther from the wall by placing the shadow closer or farther from the vine.

Leaf Veins

It's probably overkill to paint veins onto every single leaf of a huge tree, but this extra detail certainly adds interest to a focal point or to the foreground layer of a mural. There are two traditional ways to stencil veins:

One is simply to use a stencil overlay that paints a branched vein on top of the leaf (1, 2). The other way is to leave the leaf stencil in place and put a curved edge of paper or Mylar over it so that the edge makes a line connecting stem and tip of leaf. Then, with a small stencil brush, rub a small amount of color along the curved edge (3, 4).

The freehand approach is to use a very fine brush or a liner bottle to draw vein lines over the leaf (5, 6).

Special Effects

Stamens, Stems and Tendrils

1

2

These details can be stencilled in to finish and tie together a composition, but they often look better done in a rather loose freehand way. Liner bottles are great for adding stamens to flowers (1) and for making fine tendrils. For thicker stems and vines, use a liner brush with a translucent mix of paint, glaze and water. Drag the brush along, twisting and rotating as you go (2). The glaze makes it slow-drying, so if you don't like the result, simply wipe it off and start again.

Backgrounds

Painting the View

Many of the projects in this book use stencilled windows, and that means having to paint the "view" seen through the panes. It's possible to stencil a simple landscape, but you can often get a more dynamic effect with a loose, impressionistic band of sky colors.

If you don't think you are capable of this, try the following exercise. First, spend some time observing the range of emotion and color of a real sky. Now check out some books on watercolor landscape painting: note the colors and styles of the skies.

Set out a dozen sheets of paper, some big brushes and some paint (all those colors you saw in paintings and in nature). If you have any acrylic glaze, you can use it to make your paints more transparent and blendable if you want. Without planning what you are going to do, think sky and start brushing washes of color onto a page in patches and bands, blended or not. Do it quickly. Try something different on a fresh page. Do at least half a dozen pages (1).

Now cut a window template out of a fresh sheet of white paper or card stock. Place the template over those sheets of messy color (2). Do you have skies or what! Also, remember that as soon as you stencil a snippet of greenery peeking over the sill, it breaks up the sky and relegates it to a less noticeable background role.

If you ask a dozen decorative painters how to paint a sky, you'll probably get a dozen different answers. This is what works for me. I always start with a white basecoat. Then I add several layers of translucent color. Sometimes I leave white gaps for clouds; sometimes I add clouds afterward.

My translucent color medium is a mixture of acrylic glaze or extender, latex paint and water (in roughly equal parts). If I'm using this medium with a stencil, I omit the water. As for colors, I confess that I'm not as adventurous as I encourage everyone else to be. My usual skies are either blue or blue at the top, blending into various pastels toward the bottom. Maybe this is because I live in a gray, rainy climate. My clouds are soft and white, sometimes with raw umber shadows.

If I'm striving for a really impressionistic effect, I apply the sky medium in a random manner with a big paintbrush, leaving the brush strokes visible. For more subtle variations of color, soften the brush marks with cheesecloth or a blending brush. Blending must be done quickly because the sky medium has a short open, or working, time.

For a more evenly colored sky, use a large roller (use a foam roller if the sky is being painted through a stencil). Try to minimize lap lines, either by blending them in or by covering them with clouds.

Hard-edged clouds can be painted, sponged or stencilled with latex paint. For softer clouds—like puffy cotton candy, wispy cirrus or soft morning mist—add some acrylic glaze to the paint so that you can blend the edges of the clouds right into the sky colors.

Remember that whenever you do a sky through a stencil, you must be careful not to overload your brush or roller, allowing the paint to bleed under the stencil.

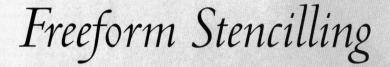

Freeform Stencilling

"I don't think necessity is the mother of invention; invention, in my opinion, arises directly from idleness, possibly also from laziness. To save oneself trouble."
—*Agatha Christie,* An Autobiography

Stencils as Building Blocks

Basic Freeform Method

Layering Without Masks

Layering With Masks

Composition

I used to think I needed an eight-foot stencil to paint an eight-foot tree. But the idea of cutting an eight-foot stencil was discouraging, and the thought of manipulating an eight-foot stencil even more so. Since I wanted a bridgeless tree, that meant I needed eight-foot overlays as well. Given my lack of skill with an artist's brush, the alternative prospect of painting the tree freehand was equally unattractive.

What stencils are *really* good for is making repeated prints of the same image, and if ever there was a repeatable element, I reasoned, a leaf was it. By stencilling the same small branch of leaves over and over with an implicit overall shape, I wound up with a reasonable facsimile of a tree. My pieced-together tree served me well—I was able to work it into corners and over doorways with an ease that would have been impossible using a gigantic stencil. Ten years later, this approach has become widespread. It even has a name: freeform stencilling.

Many of us were drawn to stencilling because the results are so predictable: Plop down a stencil, rub on some paint, and you have a perfect image. In freeform stencilling, though the technical aspects of paint application are identical, more creative input is demanded of the stenciller—and the results are never the same. Currently, it is the fastest-growing area in the whole stencilling field. Stencillers are looking for something a little more challenging than merely plunking down one repeated print after another to make a simple border.

As the name implies, freeform stencilling abandons the traditional characteristic of repetition at evenly spaced intervals. Instead, stencil prints are grouped and overlapped at the stenciller's discretion, creating a unique composition—it might be a rambling vine with tangled overlapping foliage but no recognizable repeats; it could be a lush and abundant bouquet overflowing a stone urn; or it could be something completely abstract. The finished results look more like freehand painting than stencilling, and the applications are endless—this technique can be used on everything from furniture panels to entire murals.

Freeform stencilling is the basis for almost all the examples in this book. There are three parts to the method:

▷ Repeated overlapping of small-stencil components— a leaf, a branch, a flower, a clay pot—to build up painted scenes that are unique and complex yet require no more than a modest stencilling ability. For example, by overlapping, rotating and flipping a single leafy branch stencil and using a few different colors, you can create a bush or a tree. With a leaf, a flower and a clay pot, you can paint a shelf of potted plants.

▷ Use of masks to help build up depth and complexity in your composition. For example, by placing a mask over a grape leaf, you can stencil a cluster of grapes peeking out from under it without getting burgundy paint on the leaf.

▷ Deciding, before you begin, how your final composition will grow from a few small stencils. For example, what path do you want a vine to take in meandering across a wall? Will the leaves hang down or branch upward?

The key to making all this work is to think in terms of layers. By layering stencil prints and altering your colors appropriately, you can create the illusion of background, middle ground and foreground. To stencil a really lush plant, for example, you can build up three or four layers of foliage by making overlapping leaf prints in changing hues of green. You can make the layers more distinct by using a mask to cover up one layer while stencilling an "underlapping" layer. For instance, incorporating a jumbled cluster of flowers into a stencilled bouquet is easy if you mask out the brightest foreground blossoms before adding the more subdued flowers in the background.

Masks are particularly useful when you make a big shift in colors between layers; they let you layer complementary colors, for example, without producing a muddy result.

Layering Without Masks

Transparent Layers

When you are overlapping layers of leaves, you don't always have to hide the background parts. In fact, you may want to make the foliage look translucent by allowing overlapped leaves to show through the ones on top. However, an entire garden scene will look overly busy if everything is transparent, and you will have problems where complementary colors overlap. There are a couple of ways you can do this without going to the trouble of using masks. These methods work as long as there are no dramatic color shifts among the leaves.

Because stencilling is done with such thin layers of paint, overlapping prints are usually transparent, unless you are using solid paints, scrubbing really hard with your stencil brush or intentionally building up an opaque layer of paint. To increase the transparency of acrylic and latex paints, add a small amount of acrylic glaze or extender. Using a foam roller helps as well, because it doesn't disturb any overlapping images.

A leafy branch like this one (1) often looks good in transparent colors—as though sunlight is streaming through the leaves and a soft breeze is ruffling them.

Creating a mop of hydrangea blossoms is a good exercise in overlapping stencil prints. Each individual blossom is formed by overlapping crisscrossed pairs of translucent petals (2). The mop is created by overlapping two clusters of blossoms. The first is pale blue. The second, which is stencilled on top of the first, is a brighter blue (3). In the final result, pale blossoms can be seen around the edges of the mop and in the gaps between the brighter flowers (4). When the cluster is complete, you can add centers to selected blossoms.

1

2

3

4

Layering Without Masks

Opaque Layers

◆ Method 1

This method uses latex or acrylic paint and works well with one or two layers. Beyond that, the leaves look as if they are merging into one heavy mess of green.

▷ Start with the background layer.

▷ Stencil the first leaf (1) using a cool green applied with a stencil brush or a foam roller. This will be the background leaf (i.e., the leaf that will be partly covered by the next leaf).

▷ Place the stencil so that it overlaps the first leaf at an angle (2).

▷ Stencil the second leaf using warmer, brighter greens and making sure that the leaf's edges show up against the color of the background leaf (3).

◆ Method 2

This method also uses latex or acrylic paint but will work for any number of layers.

▷ Start with the foreground layer.

▷ Stencil the first leaf (foreground) using latex or acrylic paint and a brush or a foam roller (1).

▷ To slip a second leaf behind the first one, place the stencil so that it overlaps the first leaf at an angle (2).

▷ Stencil the second leaf so that the paint fades away as it approaches the edge of the first leaf (3). Some of the second-leaf color may get on the edge of the first leaf, although it should be faint enough that it won't really show up. If it does, simply restencil the first leaf to clean it up.

◆ Method 3

This method uses the slow-drying solid stencil paints. It relies on the fact that these paints smudge when fresh.

▷ Start with the background layer.

▷ Stencil the first leaf using a brush, a swirling rather than a stippling application and a cool, somewhat pastel-green paint (1). This will be the background leaf. (If you have only one green, add some blue to make it cooler or some yellow to warm it up.)

▷ Place the stencil so that it overlaps the first leaf at an angle (2). Be careful not to smudge the print.

▷ Stencil the second leaf (again swirling instead of stippling) with a darker, warmer green (you need enough difference between the greens for the two leaves to look distinct). As your brush rubs around, it will also smudge out the part of the first leaf that shows through the stencil, because the paint hasn't dried yet and is still very blendable.

Layering With Masks

Mylar/Paper Mask

The overlapping techniques just described do not work well if the colors of the different layers tend to muddy each other when mixed. In this case, you want to stencil the foreground elements first, then protect them with a mask while you add background elements. This is not as much work as it sounds. Remember that you are making repeated use of a small number of modest-sized stencils, so you need only a small number of modest-sized masks. You will use them over and over again, just like the stencils.

I have masks for medium to large flowers, such as tulip, iris and rhododendron, some of the larger leaves, such as grape leaves, and planters and vases. The latter allow me to add plant elements that seem to be drooping down behind the vase. For rhododendrons, my stencils create the individual blooms that make up a rhododendron cluster, so my masks are also for individual blooms. This lets me create clusters that are different every time.

I don't usually bother masking small stuff. It's too much work, and small masks always get lost. If I absolutely must mask off some little shape, I use liquid frisket (see next section).

To be effective, a mask must be quite accurate. To make one, use a stencil print as your pattern. Lay a piece of thin Mylar over the pattern, and cut it out carefully. I use 3-mil Mylar because it is easy to cut and the mask doesn't have to be strong.

With single overlay stencils, you have a perfect mask: simply save the piece cut out when making the stencil. Some commercial stencils leave this piece in place to use as a mask.

Store your masks carefully (they get lost easily, especially the Mylar ones), and they will last a long time.

This example shows how to use a grape-leaf mask to stencil a cluster of grapes half hidden by a leaf.
▷ Position the masks carefully over the leaves (1). Hold in place with low-tack tape or stencil adhesive (although if you ever need to use the flip side of the mask, you may want to forgo the adhesive).
▷ The first grape prints are done with the stencil overlapping the leaf masks (2). This lets you do partial grapes without getting burgundy paint on the leaves.
▷ Finish the grape cluster with additional overlapping grapes using one of the "no-mask" overlapping methods (3). Make the grape sizes smaller as the cluster tapers.
▷ When the cluster is finished, lift the leaf masks (4).

Liquid Frisket Mask

I

Liquid frisket is a little bit like rubber cement. You paint it over the area you need to protect, let it dry, then stencil whatever you want to add to the area. When the stencil paint is thoroughly dry, you peel off the frisket. Several brands of liquid frisket are available; look for them at your art-supply store or wherever watercolor materials are sold.

This technique requires a little practice, so try it out on a sample first. Follow the instructions on the label. This sample will also act as a test to make sure that your brand of liquid frisket does not leave a stain on your work.

Liquid frisket is more time-consuming to use than are pre-cut masks, so I use it only in one-off situations or where, for whatever reason, I cannot easily make a cutout mask. In this example, I use it with hydrangea blossoms to add some leaves behind the flower cluster. I left the leaves out at first because I wanted to stencil the flowers over a white background so that the blues would stay nice and clear. The way in which the flower cluster is put together—stencilling one pair of petals at a time—means that each flower cluster is always unique. It's not worthwhile cutting out such a complicated mask if you use it only once, so this is where you bring out the liquid frisket:

2

3

4

▷ Stencil a cluster of hydrangea blossoms. Let the paint dry thoroughly (1).
▷ With a frisket tool (available where you buy liquid frisket), paint the frisket over the blossoms you need to protect (2). You could also use a small, inexpensive artist's brush to apply the frisket, but the special tool makes the application easier and produces better results. Let the frisket dry.
▷ Place the leaf stencil over the blossoms (3), and paint (4), making sure that you don't accidentally paint over any unprotected flowers.
▷ Remove the stencil (5). When the paint is completely dry, carefully rub off the frisket, following the instructions on the label.

5

Ad Hoc Mask

Sometimes, you need a quick one-time-only mask for a single edge. Cut a few scrap pieces of Mylar into curved and geometric shapes, keep them in your tool bag, and retrieve them when needed. They are also useful for repairing a smudged edge. For a quick straight-edged or right-angled mask, low-tack Post-it notes are really handy.

Composition

Plant Profiles

Mastering the technical part of freeform stencilling means learning how to stencil individual leaves and flowers, how to layer the prints effectively and how to use masks when needed. The artistic part involves deciding how to put everything together and paying attention to the way real plants grow. This part is really important. But it's not that difficult if you get inspirational help from books, magazines and nature.

Artists who take up stencilling have an advantage, because they are trained to observe. Stencils can certainly help those who "can't draw" become creative, but they won't necessarily lend the work that spark of reality which comes from a keen eye and an understanding of the subject's essential features.

Beginners of freeform stencilling often fail to pay attention to structure. They might be able to stencil perfect wisteria leaves, but if the leaves are placed without much thought as to how they should connect (1), the results will be less successful than if they seem to stem from a common branch (2).

Before stencilling any plant, make a small sketch that outlines its general profile. Decide whether the branches will be hanging or upright, the leaves alternate or opposite, the berries single or in clusters. Think of the sketch as the framework upon which you hang stencilled prints, and use it as a guideline while you work. It doesn't have to be a work of art, just enough to indicate how the plant parts are interconnected.

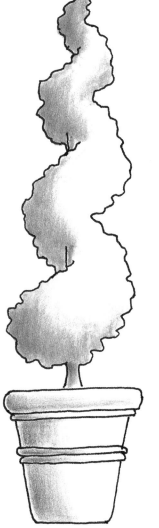

Plant Groupings

Putting together a bouquet, a planter or a hanging basket doesn't require as much of a reality check as creating a plant itself, because even in real life, it's a process of invention. However, I still find it enormously helpful to scan books on gardening, flower arranging and garden accessories, just to find the inspiration that keeps each project from looking like a clone of a previous one. I visit my local library at least twice a week, and I've probably checked out every book on flowers, trees and container gardening at least once. You never know what might spark an idea. Besides, lugging 20 pounds of books back and forth every two days really helps my 200-meter freestyle time.

I collect sketches and photocopies of profiles that I can follow when stencilling bouquets or full planters. It saves time when deciding how to incorporate various botanicals, and it gives me a ready supply of options when I'm trying to fit a composition onto, say, long, narrow bifolds or a short, fat cupboard door.

Proofs

When I'm building up a garden scene, I probably spend more time trying to decide where to stencil each leaf than I do in actually stencilling it. Should this flower be a quarter of an inch more to the left or right? Up or down? Do I want that fern to come in front of the tulip or behind it? It does help to do a sample composition on paper first, then when you have something close to what you want, you simply copy it, making any minor changes as you go. It's like writing a draft essay, editing it, then making a final clean copy to hand in. (You may also find, as I often do, that when you are doing only a draft version, your work is much freer and sometimes turns out better than the final version.)

Another device that helps you build your composition is a Mylar proof of every stencilled component. You simply stencil each leaf and flower shape onto separate sheets of frosted Mylar (the paint adheres to the frosted side). Then hold them up against your work (which will show through the unpainted parts of the Mylar), and move them around until you find just the right spot. Now you simply put the appropriate stencil in the same place.

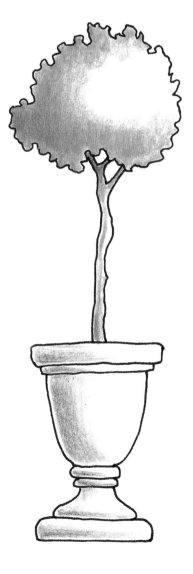

Starting Small

◇

"Painting's not my hobby; it's my spiritual retreat."
—Kate Langdale

◇

Stencilling Without Stress

Easy Freeform Projects

When I was 11 years old, my father offered me $10 to paint our house during the summer holidays. Over the years, the original linseed-oil finish on the cedar siding had weathered to a very dark brown—almost black on the north side—and we had decided that the house would look better white. Ten bucks! I was over the moon—it would double my bank account.

Looking back, I think my parents might have tried to temper my enthusiasm a little by helping me understand the magnitude of the job. But at the time, all I could think about was the money. There was nothing intricate involved with the job, I reasoned; it was just a matter of painting flat boards. How hard could that be?

But after the first half-hour of trying to scrub thick, smelly paint onto that rough, dark cedar, my excitement predictably took a nosedive. After a week, it completely bottomed out. I turned the job over to my father, and I took a 30-year hiatus from my painting career.

I still take on projects that are beyond my scope, and the experience continues to be an emotional roller coaster. I get carried away by some new idea, then grow morose when it doesn't seem to be working. When the next step in the process turns things around, my euphoria returns. Often, something that looks wonderful late at night fares poorly under the analytical light of day. Inversely, the optimistic lighthearted morning start to a project can turn desperate as time evaporates in the evening.

My problem is that once I've done something, I know it can be done, so I want to move on to something new. It's like opening a cookbook and picking a recipe you've never tried before when you're having a big dinner party for people you don't know well. In fact, almost every project I do is either something I've never done before or something that caused so much hysteria the first time around, I can't remember how I eventually got it to work.

Creative work doesn't have to be quite so stressful. E.F. Schumacher was referring to economics when he coined the phrase "small is beautiful," but it applies to decorative painting as well. I should follow my own advice: Start off small and gradually work up to more and more ambitious projects, with lots of sample boards and test runs in between. In other words, try stencilling parrot wrapping paper before tackling a jungle mural.

Greeting Cards and Postcards

Paper projects are the easiest and least expensive way to work into freeform stencilling. And cards are the easiest of paper projects. Instead of stencilling directly onto blank greeting cards, I prefer to stencil my images onto small pieces of quality paper (usually scraps I get free from my printer), which I then mount onto the blank greeting cards. This way, if I goof, all I waste is a small piece of paper. It also allows me to use additional layers of decorative paper to create a matting effect.

You can trim your papers with a knife and a straight edge or tear them into abstract shapes. Another variation is to cut a window into the card stock and mount the stencilled paper behind it.

Don't forget postcards, either. Strathmore Paper Company sells them blank in tear-off pads of 10; they are made of high-quality watercolor card stock, which is wonderfully receptive to stencilling. The reverse side is preprinted with lines for address and message.

◆ **Materials**
▷ Blossom and leaf stencils
▷ Two ½-inch stencil brushes
▷ Acrylic or latex paints (I used two greens and a soft burgundy red)
▷ Clear acrylic glaze or extender (a very small amount keeps brushes supple and makes the red slightly transparent)
▷ Scrap pieces of good-quality white or ivory paper for stencilling.
▷ Pieces of colored or hand-made paper for decorative layers
▷ Blank cards with envelopes or Strathmore blank postcards
▷ Adhesive

◆ Method

▷ Following the directions in the previous chapter for overlapping and grouping stencil prints, stencil two or three blossoms and a cluster of leaves on blank paper.

▷ When stencilling the flowers, build up a little more color around the edges and try to keep it slightly transparent. Use a light touch so that any overlapping petals show through.

▷ Stencil some overlapping leaves around, under and over the flowers, using a warmer green for foreground leaves. Cards should be done quickly and spontaneously, so don't go to the trouble of masking flowers or leaves.

▷ Trim or tear the edges of the stencilled paper to make it an inch or two smaller than the blank greeting card. Make several variations of your composition, then pick the ones you like best.

▷ Cut or tear pieces of colored or handmade paper about half an inch longer and wider than your print. Center the print on these accent papers, and glue in place with adhesive or double-sided tape.

▷ Position the print and accent papers on the front of the card, and glue in place.

▷ As a finishing touch, stencil a single blossom or leaf on the back of the envelope, centered across the opening edge of the flap.

47

Easy Freeform Projects

Paper Boxes

Decorated boxes such as this make exquisite packages for small, special gifts. Fashioned from thin poster board, they cost almost nothing but your time to make. The ones shown here are triangular, but it is easy to find patterns for other shapes. (For example, Dover Publications has a book of cutout-and-paste boxes in a dozen styles, and American Traditional Stencils sells Mylar templates for making similar boxes.)

◆ Materials
▷ Box pattern
▷ Sheet of white poster board
▷ Pansy stencil
▷ ½-inch stencil brushes
▷ Paints: blue, greens, yellow, black

◆ Method
▷ Trace box pattern onto wrong side of poster board. Cut out carefully with scissors or a utility knife (use a metal-edged ruler to guide the knife). Score all fold lines using a ruler and a knitting needle or the dull side of a blade.
▷ Turn right side up, and stencil several overlapping pansies, as shown. Each set of petals should be shaded so that they are darkest on the bottom and lightest on the top. This gradation is needed to make the petals distinct from one another.
▷ Use overlays to add the yellow center and black face. (Yellow tends to be very transparent, so you might have to add some white to make it more opaque.)
▷ Fold the three faces of the poster board to form the box. Glue the long flap. Fold and tuck the short end flaps in place.

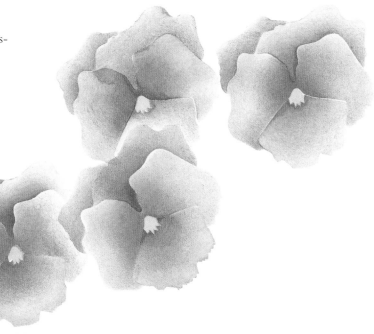

Lampshade

Kraft-paper and handmade paper lampshades can be found almost everywhere today, and they make appealing objects for stencilling. They are available in several sizes and styles. The easiest to stencil are those with the largest diameter, because curves can be a bit tricky when it comes to holding down the stencil. For this reason, try to avoid large stencils when you are working on curved surfaces.

◆ **Materials**
▷ Brown-paper lampshade
▷ Ivy-leaf stencils
▷ Paints: greens, brown
▷ Acrylic glaze or extender
▷ Stencil brushes
▷ Liner brush

◆ **Method**
▷ Try a few ivy compositions on paper until you find one you like that fits the shape of the lampshade.
▷ The easiest way to do this particular project is to use freezer-paper stencils with stencil adhesive to hold them in place, because the freezer paper molds easily to the curve. You can use Mylar stencils if you have someone to help keep them positioned. Or you can use tape in addition to stencil adhesive.
▷ Copy your trial composition as closely as possible, using a variety of greens and shading the edges of each leaf so that it looks distinct from the leaves it overlaps.
▷ Mix a little green and brown paint with some glaze and a bit of water. Load the liner brush with this mixture. Add some freehand vines and tendrils to your composition by dragging and rotating the liner brush while varying the pressure.

Place Mats

One-of-a-kind canvas place mats give you a chance to practice freeform stencilling as well as floorcloth technique in miniature—and they make great gifts.

◆ **Materials**

▷ Place-mat-sized piece of primed canvas

▷ Acrylic or latex paint: white, sky blue, greens, purple

▷ Various stencil brushes; a high-density foam roller

▷ Morning glory stencil; lattice stencil (you can substitute wide painters' tape for the lattice stencil if necessary)

▷ Acrylic varnish

◆ **Method**

▷ Cover the entire place mat with an even coat of white paint. Let dry thoroughly.

▷ Position lattice stencil, and hold in place with stencil adhesive. If you don't have a lattice stencil, lay down a diagonal grid of 1½-inch painters' tape.

▷ Roller stencil the entire grid with a pale sky blue. Stipple in cloud colors as well if you wish.

▷ With the lattice stencil still in place, stencil pieces of the morning glory vine. These pieces will appear to be behind the lattice.

▷ Remove all stencils (and tape).

▷ Stencil strips of shadow along the edges of the lattice slats.

▷ Stencil additional morning glory vine on top of the lattice, using stronger colors.

▷ Let everything dry for several days, then apply three coats of acrylic varnish.

▷ You can hem the mat if you wish by folding under the edges and gluing in place, or you can leave it unhemmed as long as the edges have been sealed with paint and varnish.

Floorcloth

Once you have tried a small version of a floorcloth, in the form of a place mat, this won't be any harder. It will just take up a little more space, a little more paint and a little more time. For this one, I started by sponging and blending an antiqued-yellow background before stencilling freeform clematis vines in a wandering pattern. I used overlapping prints of an ordinary vine border stencil to lay out the general path of the vine, then added extra leaves and flowers to fill in the composition. The colored border, which was masked off with painters' tape, was stencilled at the end. The advantages of using a freeform design such as this one are that there is no need for measuring, there's no wrong place for anything and you don't have to worry about wrapping borders around the corners. After the paint had cured, the floorcloth was finished with multiple coats of acrylic varnish.

Pine Hutch

This pine hutch is from my favorite local source of unfinished furniture. Its design lends itself beautifully to stencilling, because the center panels of each door are removable. The original idea was that you could replace them with glass panels if you wanted, but it also means that you can stencil them at the kitchen table without having to maneuver an entire piece of furniture. This makes it easier to handle the stencils too, because you don't have to try to fold them down into the corners.

◆ **Materials**

▷ A piece of undecorated furniture with a panel door that just begs to be stencilled. It can be new or recycled, unfinished or painted—a hutch, a kitchen cupboard, a bedside table or a medicine cabinet.

▷ Stencils for the leaves and fruit of a grapevine

▷ Large stencil brush for leaves; ½-inch stencil brush for grapes

▷ Acrylic or latex paints: greens for leaves, purple or burgundy for grapes

▷ Paint or stain the piece first if desired. I left mine plain. If you want to make it look as though it's been around for a while, you can also antique or crackle it. You can buy a kit to help you do this at almost any paint store.

◆ **Method**

Practice your composition first on a sheet of paper. Draw a rectangle the size of your panel on the paper to be sure the composition will fit comfortably. Once you are happy with it, you can reproduce it on the panel.

▷ Stencilling the leaves and grape clusters is a direct application of the masking techniques described in "Freeform Stencilling." Veins have been added to the leaves by running a brush along a curved Mylar edge, as described on page 31.

▷ To make the grapes look as though they are hanging underneath the leaves, protect the leaves with masks before stencilling the grapes.

▷ To build up a bunch of grapes, stencil one or two complete circles, with large ones toward the top and a few small ones near the bottom. Use a small brush (½-inch or ⅜-inch), and rub most of the color around the perimeter of each circle. This will make the grapes look somewhat three-dimensional. The centers should look transparent.

▷ Now add partial circles to build up the cluster. These circles should seem to be overlapped by the first full ones you did; lighten up on the brush pressure as the brush encroaches upon the space taken up by an overlapping grape. This will prevent it from being overpainted.

▷ When you finish the cluster of grapes, go back and restencil a few of the foremost grapes to give them a little more definition.

▷ If you want to get really fancy, highlight a few grapes by adding a dab of white paint with a small brush.

Easy Freeform Projects

Wall Border

For this project, we take a standard border stencil (a honeysuckle vine) and demonstrate two ways of moving toward producing a mural-like decoration. The trick here is to start with some kind of standard framework around which you can build up clusters of stencilled vine. The first example uses a real piece of plate-rail molding; the second, a scroll design stencilled with a regular repeat.

◆**Example One**
◇ *Materials*
▷ Any vine stencil (with or without bridges)
▷ Acrylic or latex paints: greens, creamy yellow, cool red
▷ Assorted stencil brushes
◇ *Method*
▷ Stencil a few repeats of the border so that it lays out the general path you want the vine to take (i.e., above the railing, then disappearing behind it, then trailing below, and so on).
▷ Use parts of the border stencil to add extra overlapping leaves and to build up bits that branch off in other directions.
▷ Stencil pieces of vine trailing in front of the molding in a few places.
▷ Make the vine density uneven. It should thin out in some places and bunch up in others. Vary the colors as well.
▷ This vine also has honeysuckle blossoms, which I added randomly. Blossoms are stencilled first in creamy yellow. Use a ½-inch stencil brush to blend cool red accents at the end of the blossoms.

◆**Example Two**
◇ *Materials*
▷ Scroll stencil
▷ Any vine stencil (with or without bridges)
▷ Foam roller and assorted stencil brushes
▷ Acrylic or latex paints: greens, creamy yellow, cool red, white, light brown or gray
▷ Fine mechanical pencil
◇ *Method*
▷ Stencil the scroll border using a brush or a roller. Shape the scroll sections by shading the edges with light brown or gray, using a ⅛-inch brush. If you are working on a pale wall and have trouble making the white scroll show up, trace the edges of the scroll with a 0.5 mm mechanical pencil before doing the shading. This will add contrast between the scroll and the wall and will also sharpen the shadow gradation.

▷ Place the vine stencil on top of the scroll, and tape in place. Stencil most of the vine in the usual manner. In places where you would like the vine to appear to pass behind the scroll, mask that section of the scroll before painting the vine. Usually, you will have to mask only very small parts of the scroll at a time, so a Post-it note trimmed with a curved edge will do the trick if you stencil one side of the scroll and then the other. If you plan to put many leaves and flowers behind one section of the scroll, it would be worthwhile to mask that section with liquid frisket, as described in "Freeform Stencilling."
▷ Use parts of the vine stencil to add extra overlapping leaves and to extend the vine so that it appears to branch above or below the scroll.

▷ As you work along the scroll, leave some areas free of vines. Other areas should have an abundance of vines. Just make sure the pattern is not regular.
▷ Vary the intensity of vine color. You want to have some sections very faint, as though the vines are trailing off in the distance.
▷ Add blossoms, as in the first example.
▷ If you are feeling ambitious, you can also add shadows to the scroll and to selected leaves (not shown in this example).

Focus on Flowers

"How to be an artist: Take the palette from the box, squeeze some paint on it from the tubes, dip your brush into the paint, and daub the canvas with it. Rembrandt, Titian and all other great painters used this method."
—J. Edward Breslin, Quote Me

Expanding Your Repertoire

Terra-Cotta Pots

Hanging Basket

China Vase

Vases and Flowers

Topiary Trees in Pots

It was unfortunate that my sister Linda and I hadn't had a dress rehearsal when we launched our stencil-making business in 1993, but at least our inaugural exposure was local rather than national. Having received rave reviews from the Vancouver Gift Show organizers, we were given a space in the highly publicized section reserved for new businesses. As novice entrepreneurs, the preshow pep talk filled us with visions of astounding success, countless orders and lots of money.

What we *hadn't* counted on was the nervousness and the questionable judgment that can go with inexperience. So, on the morning of the first day of the trade show, there we were backing out of the driveway, when Linda suddenly noticed she was still wearing her pyjamas. That was just the beginning.

We'd been so concerned with having a funky booth that we had spent days making twig baskets, which we thought would enhance the garden theme of our stencils. But the baskets were so funky, everyone thought *that's* what we were selling. "Oh, what lovely baskets," they would say. "How much are they?" Then the frog lady, who shared the 10-foot booth with us, our stencils and her 10,000 frog-shaped bean bags, started getting really busy. We had yet to write our first order, and she was closing a deal worth $100,000 with some Asian importer. When the frog lady's clients started asking us to take their orders for frogs, all Linda and I wanted to do was get out of the public eye.

In this chapter, you'll find projects that build on the methods applied in "Freeform Stencilling." They are not more difficult, but they *are* bigger, more time-consuming and more noticeable. Turn-of-the-century American writer and journalist Ambrose Bierce once defined painting as "the art of protecting flat surfaces from the weather and exposing them to the critic." Whether that critic be a friend, a mother-in-law or a buyer at a trade show, the barbs still sting. These projects can be easily expanded or incorporated into a larger plan, but if you're not yet comfortable with the idea of a big debut for your talents, the stencils can also be used in nooks and crannies that are more or less private.

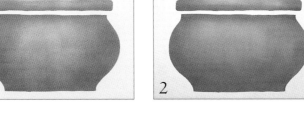

With a few good planters and a couple of great flowers in your stencilling repertoire, you can go a long way toward painting creative compositions for your wall. Perch some terra-cotta pots on a painted ledge, and "plant" them with stencilled flowers and vines. Glaze the rest of the wall in luminous blues and pastel whites, and you're looking off into a summer maritime sky; use warm pale yellows and earth tones, and it's a misty far-off Umbrian valley. If you do a good job on a small amount of foreground detail, you can often be surprisingly vague with the rest of the picture.

The planters shown on these two pages, one with perspective and the other without, were stencilled as terra-cotta containers for topiary bushes. You could use the same patterns and paint them as stone or color-glazed pottery. These pots and the simple flowerpot on the next page are stencilled in a few easy steps:

▷ Hold the stencil in place with painters' tape or stencil adhesive or both.

▷ Use acrylic or latex paint in a terra-cotta color to stencil the body and rim of the pot (1). A roller technique works well for this part because the pot is quite large.

▷ With a small stencil brush, rub some warm gray or brown color along the sides of the pot (2) and under the rim to make it look more three-dimensional.

▷ Mark the registration triangles, and replace the first stencil with the overlay. Stencil the upper-rim shadow strip and the lower rim in terra-cotta (3). Add shadow color to the entire shadow strip. Stencil highlights on the upper rim if you wish. Contour the lower rim with shadow color.

▷ Stencil the rosette in the middle of the pot with the shadow color (4) or with shadow glaze. The rosette is a simple one-piece template and requires no shading.

Once you have finished the pot, you can stencil plants in it. Here, we show two versions of a simple topiary. On this page, a leafy branch was printed repeatedly by rotating the stencil as though it were the hand of a clock: a soft green

leafy branch printed at, say, 7, 9, 11, 2 and 4 o'clock, followed by brighter overlapping branches placed at 8, 10, 12, 3 and 5 o'clock. A few berries were added with a circle template. The trunk stencil was made of two strips of torn freezer paper.

The second topiary, on the facing page, was made by overlapping repeated prints of a cluster of clematis leaves. The twisted, vinelike trunk was done with a simple one-piece stencil cut from freezer paper.

Flowerpots All in a Row

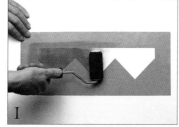

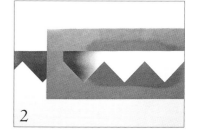

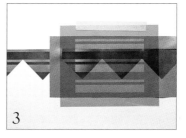

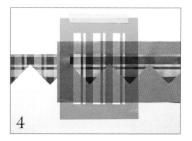

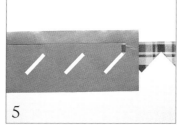

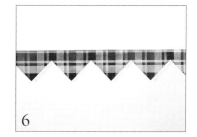

A row of stencilled pots on a stencilled shelf, opposite, makes an interesting informal alternative to a traditional border. The flowerpots are stencilled exactly the same way as the larger planter in the previous example (page 59). They are filled with a variety of stencilled herbs using the same layering technique described in "Freeform Stencilling." On this page, the pots decorate the hem of a simple piece of hanging canvas that curtains off a laundry room.

In the example on the facing page, the flowerpots have been stencilled along a fake stencilled shelf. The shelf is very straightforward, although the instructions may seem somewhat wordy:

▷ Cut a stencil for the shape of the "cloth" that hangs over the front edge of the shelf. I've used a zigzag edge cut from freezer paper, but a scalloped edge works well too. (Save the piece you cut from the stencil. You can use it later as a mask for adding a shadow.) Mark a horizontal line on the wall as a guideline for the top edge of this stencil.

▷ Use a stencil roller to fill in the basecoat of the shelf overhang (1). I've used a deep blue latex paint.

▷ To avoid lap lines when you move the stencil over for the next repeat, taper the paint to make it fade off as you reach the end of the stencil. Then, when you move the stencil over (2), place it so that the first one or two zigzags extend over the last part you stencilled— the part that you let fade away. As you stencil this next section, work your color softly into this tapered part and bring the

depth of color up to the rest of the border.

▷ When the basecoat is finished, go back to the beginning and put the zigzag stencil back in place so that it acts as an overall template for the plaid stencil, which will be stacked on top of it.

▷ The plaid stencil has alternating thick and thin stripes. I used a foam roller and an off-white latex paint. Start by stencilling a set of parallel horizontal stripes. To lengthen the stripes (3), overlap the stencil as shown and continue, tapering the overlapping parts to avoid a strong lap line.

▷ Now place the same striped stencil at right angles to the first set of stripes, and paint. To add more stripes, line up the end cutouts over the last pair of stripes stencilled (4).

▷ Practice this pattern a few times before you start the project. Avoid making the stripes too dense in color. The spots where the stripes cross should show up as distinct squares more heavily colored than the stripes alone.

▷ To create a shadow of the shelf, cover the plaid zigzag with its mask, and shift the zigzag stencil down and a little to one side (5). Lightly stencil the gap this creates with transparent shadow glaze. For a diffuse shadow, either smudge the edge of the stencilled shadow or paint a freehand shadow using the same glaze. Remove stencils and masks (6).

▷ Stencil groupings of pots along this shelf. Vary the spacing. For variety, make some of them empty or add a few that are tipped over.

Hanging Basket

This white cambric window blind hides an ugly view of the house next door. The stencilled hanging basket gives it more interest than a blank white rectangle and ties in with the leafy print of the balloon curtain.

Cambric roller blinds have a very nice surface for stencilling. It's fine-grained but has lots of tooth, and it won't stretch or shrink while you are working on it. The hanging basket is the most difficult of the projects in this chapter, so do a practice run on paper before you start. There are three steps: sponging the mossy base of the basket, stencilling an abundance of foliage and flowers to fill and hang from the basket and, finally, stencilling the wire frame that holds it all together. A variation on this method is to stencil all the plants first, then mask overhanging parts with liquid frisket while you sponge the moss and stencil the wire basket.

◆ The Moss

▷ Use the stencil to mark the approximate shape of the basket frame on your work surface.
▷ Sponge several colors of mossy green acrylic or latex paint in a random pattern that is slightly larger than the basket frame (1).

◆ The Plants

▷ Start filling the basket by stencilling the plants that appear to be showing from behind the basket (2). Keep the colors light at this point. To place a couple of ivy leaves as though they are hanging in front of the moss, first stencil them in white to "white-out" that patch of moss (2). This step ensures that the ivy colors will not be affected by those of the moss.
▷ Restencil the white ivy leaves in their appropriate colors. Build up several layers of plants around the basket (3). Try not to make things too uniform. Use leaves and flowers of different shapes and colors, some hanging, some upright. Make the overall composition somewhat irregular so that you don't end up with a completely circular ball of vegetation. Don't overdo the background or make it too bright, because you want the foreground plants to show up distinctly, and this will be difficult if they have to be stencilled over dense, intense color. You can even leave a gap or two for some bright foreground flowers. The hanging basket will look fuller if the pastel background layer fills most of the gaps between the foreground plants and extends farther to the sides. It will look more three-dimensional if there is an obvious difference in intensity among the layers of your painting.

◆ Basket Frame

▷ Once you are satisfied with the overall shape, you might want to touch up some of the foreground plants, making them a little brighter or adding details such as veins or stamens. Now you can stencil the basket frame over the moss (4). Protect any overhanging plants with liquid frisket first, then position the basket stencil and paint it black using a ⅜-inch stencil brush. Leave the odd little gap unpainted so that it will look as though the moss is covering the wire.

▷ The final step is to add the cord or wire from which the basket hangs. You can make a thick cord using a stencil, or a thin cord or wire using a liner bottle and a ruler.

China Vase

A touch of perennial spring, a stencilled bouquet can sit forever on top of a radiator without wilting.

When you cut the vase stencil, save the cutout to use as a mask. Stencil and shade the basic vase, as shown in "Technical Review" (page 30). The decorative pattern is added with a simple overlay.

◆ **The Vase**
▷ Stencil the entire vase silhouette with a deep blue basecoat, contouring it by building up more color around the sides and bottom (1). I used latex paint and a foam stencil roller.
▷ Position the decorative overlay, and stencil it in white, using a stencil brush to pick out all the fine details (2).
▷ Replace the silhouette stencil, and add a little more shading by rubbing some blue around the sides and bottom, over the white pattern. You can also add freehand highlights on the upper bulge of the vase with a round artist's brush.

◆ **The Bouquet**
▷ Position the flower stencil above the vase. Use a mask or painters' tape (3) to protect the lip of the vase while stencilling the flower stems.
▷ Remove tape and stencils (4).

◆ Variations

Change the look of the vase completely by altering the color scheme illustrated at left. This one has a white basecoat, rounded with a tinge of burgundy. The overlay design has been stencilled with several colors that blend together wherever they overlap.

◆ Tulip Bouquet

Before starting, I moved the radiator cover away from the wall so that I could lay the stencils flat in place and work more easily.

I started by stencilling the vase and a group of three foreground tulips. Then I covered them with masks and added a few individual tulips to the background, using slightly more subdued colors. The final step was to add stems and leaves, again using masks wherever I wanted the greenery to pass behind a bloom. I also added a few clematis leaves to break up the linearity of the tulip foliage.

The ginger jar and lid were first stencilled completely white, with a little green shading to give them roundness. For the green pattern, I used the same overlay as for the vase.

Slight transparent shadows were added by offsetting the appropriate stencils and applying a touch of shadow glaze with a soft stencil brush.

Vases and Flowers

With a few botanical stencils, you can create endless variations of bouquet and planter themes. Changing your colors from cool to warm or from bright to pastel will completely alter the look of a composition, as will the way you group individual plants together.

The order in which the stencilled image on this page was built up is:

▷ Stencil two foreground irises and bud (flowers only).
▷ Add foreground tulip flower.
▷ Mask tulip and irises.
▷ Stencil pale iris in background.
▷ Stencil middle tulip, mask it, and stencil remaining tulips.
▷ Stencil lupinelike flowers, using upside-down wisteria stencil, masking where necessary.
▷ Stencil vase.
▷ Mask vase, and stencil stems and leaves.
▷ Remove all masks, and stencil leaves that hang in front of vase.

The image on the facing page was built up as follows:

▷ Stencil cluster of alstroemeria.
▷ Stencil hydrangea and daisies.
▷ Stencil hydrangea leaves, masking where needed.
▷ Stencil vase.
▷ Stencil leafy branches, masking flowers and vase wherever needed.

Basic Structures

*"An expert is a man who has made all the mistakes
which can be made in a very narrow field."*
—Niels Bohr, Danish physicist

Always Have a Plan B

Porch Railings

Pickets

Wrought Iron

Lattice

69

Always Have a Plan B

Porch Railings

Kitty Corner

One of the projects in this book was so easy that I left it until the very end because I knew it required so little thought. But when you're halfway through a week of an expensive photo shoot and have been up every day at five in the morning and never in bed before midnight, and there are five people in the studio counting on you to have the right set ready when needed—well, even Jell-O can fail.

So there I was at 11 o'clock at night, scrubbing off paint, sanding down plaster and basecoating for the third time, trying to make my oh-so-simple stencil prints look right. If making mistakes is how you learn, I earned a graduate degree that night.

When my sister agreed to host her niece's wedding, she had a momentary lapse of sanity: At the last minute, she offered to paint a garden mural for a backdrop. On the day of the big event, there she was in fancy dress and high heels, frantically touching up stencils as the guests were coming up the walk.

In times of crisis, you need a fallback strategy, something you can count on, like a security blanket or chocolate-chip macadamia-nut cookies—or an easy, repeatable lattice stencil that makes a wall look "muralled" in no time. No one has to know that you'd planned to re-create the hanging gardens of Babylon. If the wedding starts in an hour and a half, stencil a big bunch of clematis in the corner, and leave it at that.

Fences, lattices and other structural forms make ideal fallback stencils for big projects, providing straightforward, easy repeats that add pattern to a large area in relatively little time. They can be either embellished to the hilt or left alone. If you're pressed for time or are running low on creative energy, you can even do the fence now and add the tulips later without the whole thing looking like an unfinished piece of work in the meantime.

An intermediate project like this builds your confidence and helps your level of expertise catch up with your aspirations. To make it easier, you can leave out the balusters; I included them as a visual extension of the existing stair railing.

A small composition can often be more appropriate than a mural that fills the entire wall, especially if there is a lot of furniture in the room. It's perfect for a child's room—in a play corner or next to the bed.

◆ **Foreground Layer: in front of the balusters**

I stencilled the cat before anything else, because I wanted to do it on a nice clear background. Then I covered it up with a mask until everything else was finished.

▷ The cat uses three overlays. Stencil the first (head and feet) in white or a buff color (a roller works well here), then use a medium (⅝-inch) stencil brush to add a little yellow ocher and brown shading around the edges. Don't forget to pencil the registration marks before lifting the stencil.

▷ The second stencil adds the facial details (1). Do this one all in black with a stencil brush.

▷ Position the third overlay. Stencil the irises of the eyes: do them first in white, then yellow, because yellow is too transparent to cover black. For the rest of the body, add calico colors in patches. Start with the lightest color (yellow ocher), and cover most of the body. Stipple and stroke patches of brown to overlap some of the ocher and to fill in any blank spots (2). Finally, shade the top of the cat's back with black, and add some black patches to the body (3). Do not overblend the colors.

▷ Shield the cat by covering it with a paper or Mylar mask.

◆ **Background Layer: behind the balusters**

▷ Stencil a bush behind the cat using a simple leaf-cluster stencil. With the cat protected by a mask, place the leaf stencil as shown (4) and paint with a roller-stencilling method. Build up the shape of the bush with repeated overlapping prints of the stencil. Try to create subtle differences in color and intensity between the layers of leaves (5).

▷ Add veins or blossoms if you wish. I expanded this painted garden by stencilling a patch of foxgloves and a small tree as well. (I added the brightest foliage after stencilling the stair railing, using a mask to block out the balusters.)

◆ **The Balusters**

▷ Cut a stencil for a single baluster post. Save the cutout to use as a mask.

▷ Use tape and the roller-stencilling method to paint the upper horizontal rail. Before removing the tape, shade the lower edges. For this, I drew a thin pencil line along the edge, then smudged the line with a small stencil brush thinly loaded with shadow glaze.

▷ Roller stencil the vertical balusters below the horizontal rail. Give them some roundness by shading the edges with gray or taupe using a stencil brush. Before removing the stencil, use tape, paper or Mylar straight edges, along with a small stencil brush, to shade the horizontal grooves, as described in "Technical Review" (page 30). I had to exaggerate the shading on this whole balustrade to make it show up well against the almost white wall.

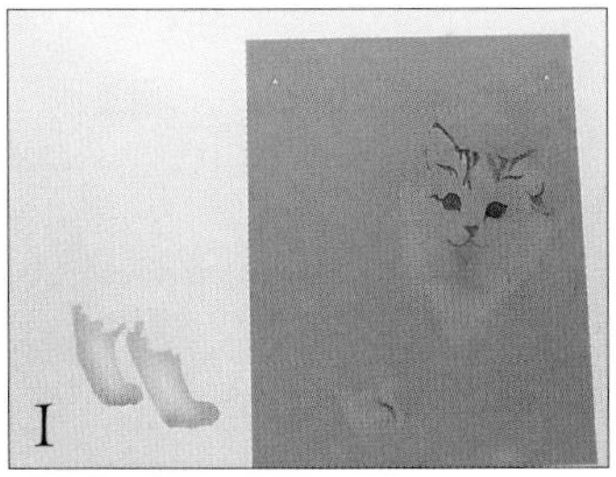
1
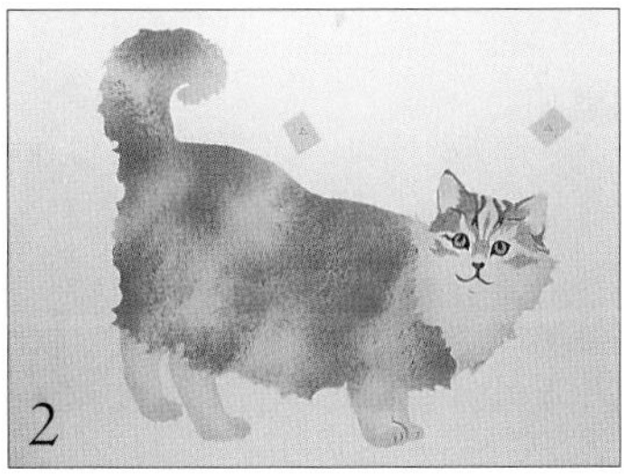
2
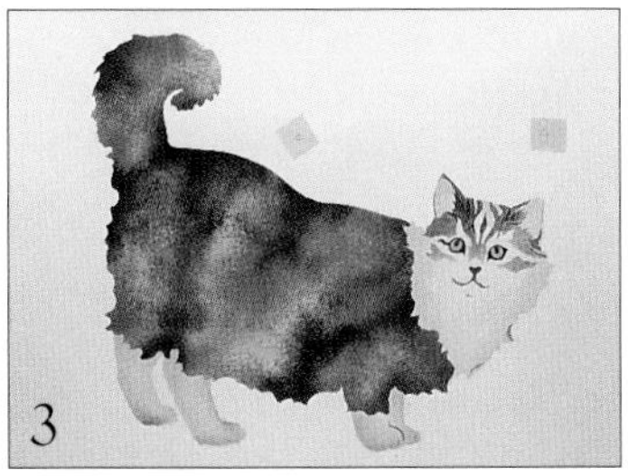
3
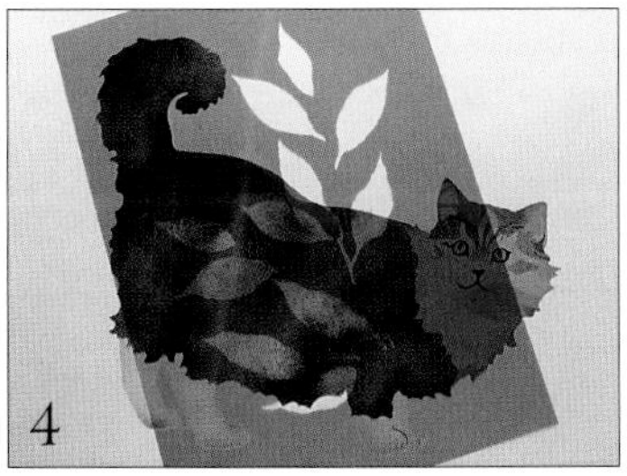
4
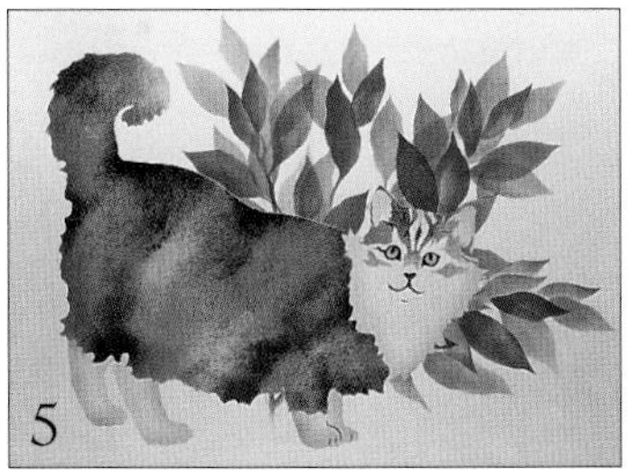
5
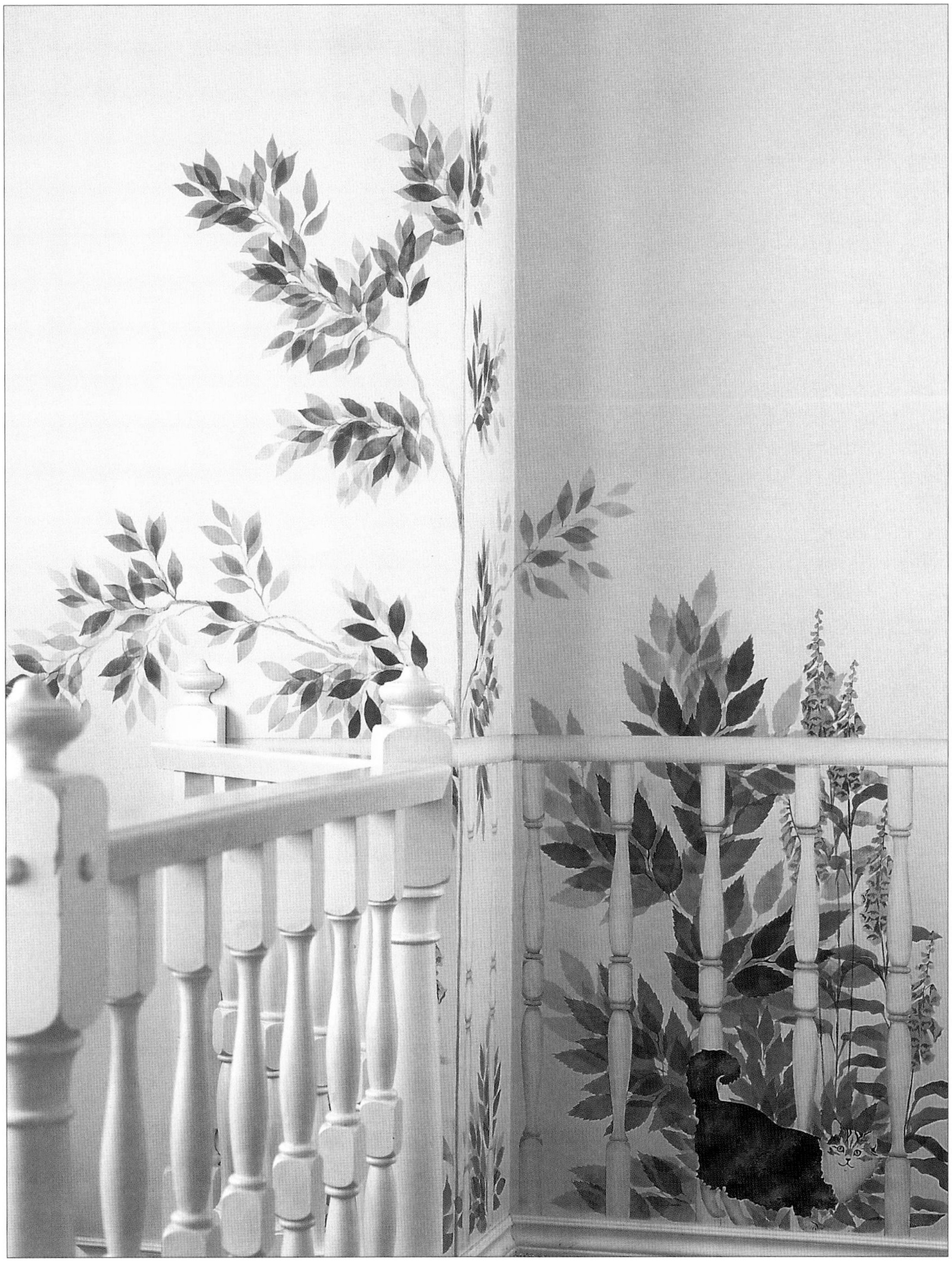

Pickets

Picket Fence

The amount of work needed to stencil this picket fence can vary a great deal, depending on whether you want to fence in an entire room, a small section of wall or just a folding screen. Make some preliminary sketches to set up the overall design, as well as a sample board to help pick plant styles and colors and to get a feeling for how the stencils work.

There are four stages: the background (an optional sky and clouds, plus pale distant elements of the landscape), the fence, the middle ground (the stuff that's in front of the background but still behind the fence) and the foreground (whatever is in front of the fence).

◆ **Background**

▷ For a quick project, stick to a plain painted background surface, but make it different in color from the fence. To be more creative, try manipulating glazes or washes of various colors to make a luminous sky. For more details on sky and cloud techniques, consult one of the many faux-finish books available in libraries and bookstores (some are listed in the Sources section).

▷ Anchor the sky with an irregular strip of pale green at the bottom of the wall (1).

▷ Fill in the most distant elements of the background—a few bushes, a tree—using the basic freeform method and very pastel colors. At this stage, you don't want to paint anything that's too bright to be easily covered over by stencilled pickets.

◆ **Fence**

▷ Measure the width of the space to be spanned by the fence, and calculate how many complete pickets will fit. Any leftover space can be incorporated into fat fenceposts painted in the corners of the room. This also eliminates having to stencil into the corner.

▷ Place a guideline of painters' tape across the space to keep your fence level.

▷ Now stencil one picket at a time across the space (2) using a roller technique and opaque latex paint. I use gesso for white fences because it's more opaque than anything else. You will probably have to stencil each picket twice, depending on how bright the background is.

▷ Stencil shadows and highlights (3).

◆ Middle Ground

▷ By masking out selected pickets (4), you can stencil brighter elements behind them. Do this until the fenced-in garden is nicely filled in and layered.

▷ By positioning a branch stencil so that it covers a masked picket, an unmasked picket and the space in between, you can make the branch look as though it is poking out in front of one picket from behind another one.

◆ Foreground

▷ Add a few small plants in front of the fence using the brightest colors.

Wrought Iron

Wrought-Iron Fence

I find wrought-iron fences easier than picket fences because I usually make them very dark, so they cover any background easily. This allows you to paint and stencil your entire scene before adding the fence. However, if you want a few pink tulips to poke in front of the iron bars, you will have to shield them with masks before you lay down the wrought-iron stencil. Alternatively, you would have to stencil the blooms with layers of white paint first to white-out the black bars, then restencil them in your chosen color.

In this example (1), a hydrangea cluster is protected by a mask held in place with stencil adhesive. With the stencil in position, the wrought-iron post is roller stencilled in black (2). Remove the stencil and mask, and you will see that the mask kept the black paint off the hydrangea, making it look as though it is in front of the post (3). To create the low stone wall, use the same technique described for the Paving Stones project in "Floors" (page 112).

A plywood folding screen is a good project for a detailed composition such as this one. It confines the composition to a limited area so that you can concentrate on making a lush picture without feeling overwhelmed by the scope of it. And it's portable—you can take it with you when you move.

Chez Piggy Fence

So where's the Piggy? you ask. Chez Piggy is a terrific little restaurant in the historic part of Kingston, Ontario. It offers an eclectic cuisine, including a divine mushroom soup that gives you at least four times the recommended daily intake of butterfat in one bowl. The building used to be a livery stable in the 1800s and was built with thick limestone walls and heavy timbered ceilings. It has a small terrace in the courtyard that's bordered with a little iron fence, which I used as the model for this stencil.

This is a perfect example of a fallback project: a simple and sparse iron fence stencilled against a terra-cotta faux finish. Roller stencilled in black, with brushed-gold highlights, this fence can cover a wall in less than an hour. In five minutes, you could add stencilled shadows, which I chose to omit here. Maybe next year, you might get around to embellishing the scene with painted foliage, maybe not. Sometimes, a simple touch is all you need.

Lattice

Basic Technique

All these lattice projects operate on the same principle. You start with a white surface. The stencil acts both as a template for painting the sky that appears through the lattice and as a mask to shield the lattice slats so that you can paint plants behind the lattice. When the lattice stencil is removed, you can add foreground plants.

◆ **Background**

This example shows a plain blue sky, but you can color it any way you want, with latex paints or acrylic glazes. The only precaution is that you must use a stencilling method of application (i.e., very small amounts of medium), or the sky will bleed under the lattice stencil.

▷ With the lattice stencil in place, apply sky color with a stencil roller (1).

▷ Keep the lattice stencil in place (2) while you stencil any foliage that is to appear behind the lattice (i.e., partially obscured).

▷ Remove all stencils.

◆ **Lattice Shadows**

▷ There are several places you can add shadows to increase the sense of realism. You can use all of them or just some, depending on how much effort you want to expend.

▷ I always make a kind of diffuse shadow cast by the upper edge of a lattice slat wherever it crosses another slat (3). I do this by protecting the foremost slat with tape or a straight piece of Mylar and making a light swipe of shadow glaze onto the overlapped slat, using a large, soft stencil brush. You use such a small amount of glaze, the bit that gets on the sky doesn't show up. This figure also illustrates a long, unbroken

shadow that you can put along the lower edge of the slats. For a small piece of work, use a stencil for this shadow. If the slats are really long, it is probably easier to use tape.

▷ Figure 4 shows a section of lattice with the diffuse shadow at the top of each slat intersection and the solid shadow along the lower edge of the foremost slats. I never bother putting this long shadow on the rear slats.

▷ If you have the time, you can use a small stencil to add the short shadows cast onto the rear slats by the lower edges of the foremost slats (5). This sounds more complicated than it actually is.

▷ The quick and easy option is to leave out the long shadows and just do the diffuse shadow at the top of every intersection along with the short, solid shadow at the bottom (6). You can cut a small piece of Mylar that will let you do both at the same time, masking the upper edge and placing a cutout below the lower edge.

◆ **Foreground**

▷ The last step is to stencil foreground leaves (7)—the ones that seem to be growing in front of the lattice. By masking a few of the slats, you can also stencil leaves so that they seem to be coming through between slats, partially hidden and partially in front.

Kitchen Lattice

Instead of covering an entire wall, this lattice simply fills in the top two feet of the wall in my kitchen, as though it were topping a garden enclosure. The sky that appears through the lattice has been continued over the ceiling, and a few of the leaves have been stencilled to extend onto the ceiling as well. Restricting the painted decoration like this saves you an incredible amount of work and also keeps the room from looking too busy.

Lattice

Lattice Room

The method for this room was basically the same as the method for the kitchen lattice, with two exceptions. Because the lattice framework was too widely spaced to use a stencil, painters' tape was applied instead. Once the framework was masked off, a blue sky and white clouds were painted over ceiling and walls, using water-based glazes for a subtle faux finish. The wisteria, morning glories and vine stem were roller stencilled, as were the swallows. The hummingbird was stencilled with a brush, blending multiple colors through the same template.

Lattice

Garden Gate

This garden gate started out as a hollow-core door, primed and painted white. A Mylar lattice stencil, combined with an arch cut from a large piece of poster board, was used to mask the upper part of the garden gate. The sky was roller stencilled with blue, pink and yellow glazes mixed with latex paint. Clouds were added by brush. Some of the honeysuckle was stencilled with the arch and lattice still shielded; brighter foreground vines were added after the lattice stencil was removed.

Attic Trapdoor Skylight

I don't know why I never thought of doing this before —it is so easy to make an attic trapdoor look like an exotic skylight. Attic covers are flat and relatively small, so they are easy to work on. I put this one on my worktable, painted it white, covered it with a fancy-shaped Mylar lattice, roller stencilled the sky and pounced the clouds. After removing the lattice stencil, I added shadows with a simple overlay. If you make a mistake, you can just say it's a bird dropping.

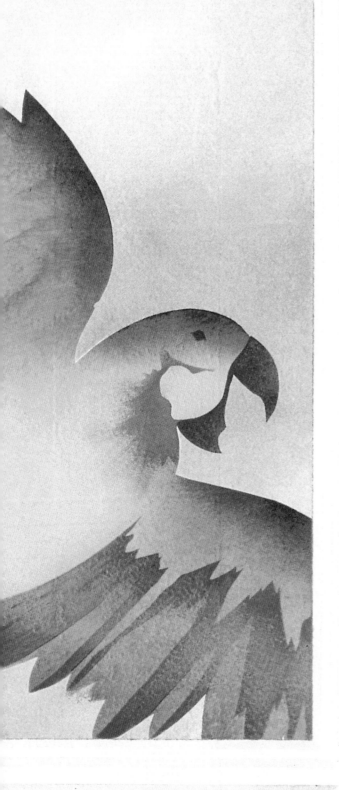

Setting Limits

◇

*"The ability to simplify
means to eliminate the unnecessary
so that the necessary may speak."*
—Hans Hofmann (painter)

◇

Masterpiece Aspirations

Making Murals Manageable

Windows

Doors

Drapery and Curtains

Windows With Curtains

When my sister Linda was 7, she thought she'd found a license to print money. Oblivious to a possible absence of artistic talent, she decided to stage a one-woman art show at 10 a.m., Saturday. It would cost 10 cents to get in and 25 cents to buy a painting. Linda sold tickets aggressively to everyone, including Miss Smith, her grade-two teacher. She made all Mom's friends buy tickets. All she had to do next was come up with the paintings.

After school on Friday, she started churning out one painting after another on our homemade plywood easel. She settled on landscapes, because that way, she wouldn't have to draw people. She also devised a foolproof formula: Tape up a sheet of newsprint. A few broad strokes of blue at the top—the sky. A narrow strip of dark blue in the middle—the sea. A band of light brown at the bottom—the shore. Untape the paper, stack it on the bed, tape up another sheet. Blue, dark blue, brown. Sky, sea, shore. Each masterpiece took just a few minutes, and that included the time spent taping and stacking.

When it comes to decorative painting, it doesn't hurt to have a formula or two up your sleeve, but that doesn't have to mean every project will look the same. Rather, it provides a simple, proven route to follow, one with which you can be completely comfortable. If time, energy and inspiration permit, you can always meander away from the road with the knowledge that as long as you can wander back again, you'll still reach your destination.

When it comes to freehand painting, most do-it-yourselfers have masterpiece aspirations, but unfortunately, their expertise and confidence are often more in line with my sister's landscape formula. However, there *is* a way to marry ambition and ability if you employ the device of fake windows and doors, expertly rendered with the help of stencils. The stencilled details of these foreground structures hold the eye, which then unwittingly integrates them with the subtle "views" painted into the windowpanes or door panes. Here, you *can* get away with simple bands for sky, sea and shore as long as the window frames are well executed. And, if you use stencils, they will be.

Reinforce the illusion by stencilling a few detailed vines, branches or flowers in the foreground just "outside" the window or by placing a stencilled flowerpot on the windowsill or adding stencilled curtains at the window. Stencilled windows are a tremendously creative device, because they allow you to give the impression of an entire mural when all you are really doing is painting or stencilling little bits of a mural, that is, whatever can be seen through the windowpanes. You never have to stencil an entire tree, only the part of a branch that hangs in front of the window.

To simplify my murals even more, I leave out any distant background. I try to design the major chunk of any "view" so that all I have to paint freehand is sky or fog. It doesn't seem to matter that most real windows or doors look out onto something more concrete—powers of logic seem to take a holiday here. A case in point is the French door on page 90. Unless your balcony is on the edge of a cliff or on the 41st floor of a high rise, there's not much chance of having a view like this. But if your brain doesn't object to not seeing the rooftops of Paris or Akbar crossing the Ganges, then why bother going to all that trouble? There's nothing like a socked-in fog for simplifying a landscape.

To avoid using lines of perspective, I try to keep the viewpoint straight on. Typically, there is no perspective to my balcony railings or stone planters, and likewise, the inside frame of the window is seen head-on. This device not only ensures that the design works but also means that the mural looks fine wherever you are in the room, whether you are sitting or standing. You don't really miss the perspective. You can look at the straight edge of the planter and get distracted by its shading and by the mass of flowers, instead of immediately thinking, "Hey, shouldn't I be looking down into that pot?"

Windows

Leaded Windows

This is one of those older three-panel doors that come with glass in the top for exterior use or with an opaque panel for interior use. Mine had a panel covered with 60 years of flaking paint. I scraped off the worst, sanded the rest and used a few stencils to make the panel appear as though it were a window looking out on a country landscape.

First, I taped off the edges of the panel, then I painted a really simple landscape, using a formula similar to the one my sister invented long ago: a stripe of greens at the bottom, a wedge of blue-greens (indicating trees) at the horizon and a big area of gray-blue for the sky. I scrubbed white and grays together to make some clouds, then added a few thin lines for a fence and a patch of green for a not very successful tree in the middle distance.

To take the observer's mind off the so-so landscape, I stencilled some tangled full-sized vines in the corner of the window, as though they are growing across the outside of the window casement. Because these leaves are big and bright, they draw the eye.

Finally, I stencilled the strips of lead that separate the panel into panes of glass, using a mix of black and silver paint with silver highlights. I used a tiny stencil overlay for the spots of solder on the junctions of the lead strips.

Windows

Simple Four-Pane Window, White Frame

As far as my own work is concerned, this is my most useful stencil. Although for reasons of size, manageability and packaging, the stencil is designed as a small four-paned window, it is really easy to use in a repeated fashion to create French doors or windows of any size. Apart from laying out the overall window placement and making sure it is level, there is virtually no measuring to do. No fiddly calculating and marking the height and width of each pane.

◆ Preparation

▷ Mark the wall where you want the top edge of the window frame to go, making sure that the edge will be level. Position the window stencil so that the top lines up with your marks. Hold the stencil in place with tape on the *inside* edges. With a fine pencil (e.g., 0.5 mm mechanical), trace the four outer edges of the stencil onto the wall. Remove the stencil, and paint the inside of the traced rectangle with white latex paint (flat or eggshell), using a foam roller to get a smooth finish and painters' tape to get clean edges. Let dry overnight.

▷ Put the window stencil back up (1), aligning it carefully with the white rectangle. Tape it firmly in place along the *outside* edges. You can also use stencil adhesive to keep the ribs from shifting. With a fine pencil, trace the outline of each pane onto the wall. It's not necessary to remove the pencil marks when you are finished. They end up being incorporated into the shadow lines.

◆ Painting the View

▷ For simplicity, these instructions refer to blue and white skies, but of course, you can substitute whatever you want. Roller stencil the windowpane cutouts with sky-blue paint or glaze (2). You can make it smooth, blended and even, dark at the top and lighter at the bottom or streaked with other colors. Various paint options for skies are discussed in "Technical Review" (page 33). Just be careful not to overload the roller and let paint bleed under the stencil. If your first pass at the sky doesn't give you quite what you want, go over it one or two more times before removing the stencil. Let the sky dry thoroughly in between each coat.

▷ If you wish to add clouds, do so with the window stencil still in place. Position the clouds to cover up any major flaws in your sky. Don't worry about minor imperfections. Remember that you will be breaking up the sky with stencilled pieces of vines or trees. These will either hide the flaws or distract the eye from them. Also, the picture always looks better after the window stencil has been removed. Lift a corner for a quick peek from time to time, and you'll see what I mean.

▷ Don't let the clouds and sky intimidate you. You can simply roll on some blue and rub on some patches of white, and it will look great, especially after you have added a few plants.

5

6

7

8

▷ Before you remove the window stencil, add any plants or vines that you want growing "outside," using the basic freeform method (3). In this instance, you might want to change the way you layer the colors, putting bright, warm colors in the background, as if they were lighted by sunshine, and using darker, cooler colors for the foreground, where the leaves might be shaded by the ones behind them.

▷ Remove the window stencil (4).

◆ **Shadows**

▷ The next step is to add shadows around the individual panes. You need two shadow colors, one deeper than the other. Choose the colors carefully—they have to show up against the window frame and against each other, but the contrast should be subtle. Mix a little glaze with the paint to make the colors slightly transparent and easy to blend.

▷ Decide where the simulated source of light will be. In this example, the light comes from the upper left, within the room, which means that the top and left edges of each pane are in shadow. This stencil creates two layers of shadow for these dark edges and narrow highlights along the other two edges. The long, thin bridge of Mylar on this stencil can shift easily, so you need to use stencil adhesive, work your brush parallel to rather than across the strip and proceed cautiously.

▷ Stencil a broad shadow at the top of each pane, using the lighter of the two shadow colors (5). At the same time, you can stencil the two narrow strips at the bottom of the panes. These strips are supposed to be highlights, but since it's difficult to find something whiter than white, I usually do them with my light shadow color, and they look just fine.

▷ Stencil the same broad shadow along the left edge of each pane and the narrow strips along the right edge (6).

▷ When the broad shadows are completely dry, stencil narrow strips on top of them, using the dark shadow color (7).

▷ The last step is to stencil shadows marking the casement for the whole window. This makes the window look slightly recessed (7). You can also add an outside shadow that makes the window frame come out from the wall a little.

▷ With a slight variation on the finishing touches, you can cut a windowsill stencil or make the window look deeply recessed by stencilling the outer edges of the window frame in shades and tints of the wall color (8). Don't forget to miter the corners.

Windows

Nonwhite Frames

If your window frame is going to be a color other than white, you must still start with a white rectangle, because there is no way to make the colors of the painted view luminous without painting over a white basecoat.

▷ Follow the instructions for the simple white framed window, but stop before you do the shadows. Cut rectangular freezer-paper masks for all the panes, and spray the back of the masks with stencil adhesive. Shield each pane with a carefully positioned mask (1).

▷ Use a roller-stencilling technique to paint all the exposed white framework in the color you want (1, 2). Be very careful to remove excess paint from your roller so that paint does not bleed under the masks.

▷ Continue with the shadow steps. In this case, you can use a highlighting color for the highlighted strips.

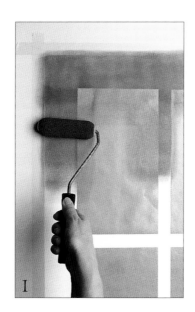

Larger Windows

To make a larger window or French doors, paint your rectangle in the appropriate size. With the four-paned window stencil positioned in, say, the top left-hand corner of the rectangle, trace the outline of each pane using a fine pencil.

Move the stencil over so that the two left cutouts line up exactly with the two outlined panes on the right. This will leave the two right cutouts of the stencil extending to the right, beyond the initial four panes that you outlined. Trace these two new panes onto the wall in pencil.

Now you have six panes outlined, in two rows of three. For an even wider window, continue in the same fashion.

To make the window taller, follow the same basic procedure, only shifting the stencil down instead of to the right. When you have finished, your initial white rectangle will be filled with an even grid of penciled rectangles, each representing a windowpane.

When it comes to using a four-paned stencil to stencil the "view" from a large window, such as the French door on page 90, it normally involves shifting the stencil a lot if the view encompasses many panes. To save myself all that work, I put the stencil aside after I have used it as a guide to pencil in the pane outlines and use one-inch painters' tape to mask off all the frames (the ribs are one inch wide). With the pencil lines as a guide, this is an easy task, with no measuring required. The tape stays on until the sky and view (here, the balustrade, planter and flowers) are finished and I'm ready to do the shadows.

Doms

French Door

For half a century, the economical flat hollow-core door has been a mainstay of affordable housing in North America. It still is. Tried, tested and…boring. However, a few stencils and a bit of paint can go a long way toward transforming it.

It's an old trick, for example, to stencil fake raised panels onto a flat door. In the previous chapter, we showed a door that had been stencilled as a garden gate. With the window stencil, you can glaze a door without buying glass. If you are not eager to put a lot of effort into painting or stencilling a "view," you can cover most of the panes with a stencilled curtain or install panes only on the top portion of the door (with a misty sky as your view). Be sure to remove the door handles before starting to paint the door.

Creating the windowpanes on this hollow-core door is a straightforward application of the basic window described earlier. Plan it on paper first to figure out how many panes to fit on the door and how wide to make the door frame.

After measuring and marking the door frame, I used my four-paned stencil as a guide to trace outlines of all the panes onto the door with a fine pencil. (I don't bother erasing the pencil tracings later. Once the sky has been stencilled, these outlines don't show up, except perhaps to make the edge of the window frame a little more crisp. This is particularly useful in defining a white frame with a white cloud behind it.)

As described on page 88, I covered the ribs of the door with one-inch painters' tape, using my pencil lines as guides. The tape stayed in place until the sky was painted and the balustrade, planter and flowers were stencilled. Then the tape was removed, and the window shadows were stencilled. You will find instructions for stencilling a stone balustrade in "Stone & Shadow" (page 125).

Veranda Door

This fake screen door is a variation on the window treatment. Here, there's only one big window, with gingerbread pieces in the corners. The veranda balusters introduce a second layer of masking before the garden can be stencilled. When you start using multiple simultaneous layers of stencils and masks, it is important to analyze where the different layers of your composition belong.

In this case, the garden goes behind everything, the balusters come next, then the gingerbread. The four masks for the gingerbread corners go on a white door first (held in place with stencil adhesive), after the edge of the door is taped off. Next in place is a mask for the balusters, again held in place with stencil adhesive.

Now you are ready to stencil the sky, the foxgloves and the hydrangea. The leaves at the top imply that there is a large tree out there somewhere. Again, I've let the view taper off into the misty distance.

Once the garden is finished, remove the baluster mask, revealing the white porch railing. Stencil rounded shading and crevices onto the railing and the white baluster posts. Remove the four gingerbread masks and the tape around the perimeter of the door. Stencil shadows to indicate paneling on the lower part of the door.

Fooling the Eye

I doubt whether there is an easier method for creating convincing trompe l'oeil curtains than this.

The idea first occurred to me when I saw two paintings by Pierre Bonnard (*La femme à la robe quadrillé* and *L'enfant au pâté*) in the Musée d'Orsay shortly after it opened in 1987. I couldn't get the image of Bonnard's flat rendering of checkered cloth out of my head, until finally, I imagined juxtaposing two pieces of his checkered pattern. Suddenly, I saw curtains!

The method works best when the "cloth" has a small, regular repeated pattern, such as a tight calico, a gingham or a plaid. You make breaks in this pattern to create the illusion of folds in the cloth.

Within each section, or fold, you stencil the pattern in a straightforward manner, as though you were making an overall pattern on a wall. When you move to stencil an adjacent section, you break the pattern by shifting it a tiny bit up or down and to one side and rotating it slightly. Once your eye hits that break, it's tricked into thinking the cloth has a fold in it. The three-dimensional illusion can be enhanced by shading the edges of each fold or by making recessed folds slightly darker, but no other artistic device is needed.

Easy Cloth Patterns

I love to use geometric cloth patterns, such as ginghams, with this method because it is so easy and because minor breaks in the pattern are so obvious. The templates are simply short segments of parallel stripes, which I roller stencil with latex paint. If you taper the paint at the end of the stripes, you can shift the stencil and make the stripes longer without lap lines. (This is demonstrated for the plaid shelf on page 60.)

For ginghams (1), stencil a set of vertical stripes over your base color. Then rotate the stripe stencil 90 degrees, and stencil an overlapping set of horizontal stripes.

You can create variations on the gingham theme by using different combinations of stripes, by alternating thick and thin stripes (2), for example.

Tartans can be done the same way, although they might involve more than one stencil, depending on the pattern you want. This tartan (3) has a red basecoat, with pairs of wide and narrow stripes stencilled in black. An overlay was used to add a narrow yellow stripe.

These patterns work fine just as they are, but if you incorporate any really wide folds in the drapery, there's one extra trick you might consider. For the ginghams and tartans, I use straight linear stencils for the warp of the cloth (i.e., the up and down of a hanging curtain) and for the woof (the crossways stripes) when it is near eye level. But for sections above and below eye level, I cut a very slightly curved version of the stencil for printing the crossways stripes (4). I use it concave up or concave down, depending on the shape of the fold.

Drapery and Curtains

Basic Method

The following steps can be used to stencil draped fabric on any scale, from a trompe l'oeil tea towel hanging on the wall to a swag spanning 20 feet. The only difference between these two projects is the size of the freezer-paper outline that you stick on the wall. And, of course, the amount of time it takes.

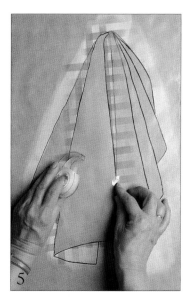

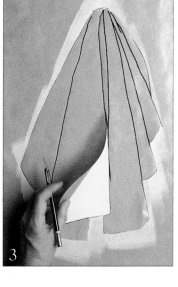

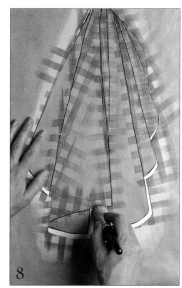

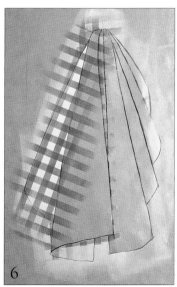

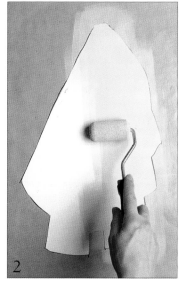

Nongeometric Drapery

▷ The outline for this hanging tea towel has been transferred to the shiny side of a large piece of freezer paper using a permanent felt pen (1).

▷ Spray the back of the freezer-paper pattern lightly with stencil adhesive, and let it dry. Position the pattern on the wall, and smooth out any wrinkles.

▷ The first step is to paint the base color of the cloth. With a very sharp craft knife, carefully cut away, in one piece, the freezer paper covering the entire towel profile. Using a roller-stencilling method, paint this exposed part with the base color of the fabric (2). You may have to apply several coats, since each one will be very thin. Let each coat dry thoroughly before recoating.

▷ Let the basecoat dry for several hours or overnight. Replace the piece of freezer paper you removed in the first step. Fit it into place exactly. Tape the edges down with Scotch tape.

▷ Cut out one section or fold of the towel pattern with a sharp craft knife (3). If the knife is sharp enough, you should be able to do this without more than a scratch on the wall.

▷ Stencil this section with the fabric pattern, orienting the pattern more or less straight up and down the section (4).

▷ Replace the freezer-paper piece over the section you just finished, taping it down with Scotch tape (5). Cut out and remove the adjacent section.

▷ Stencil this new section (6), but make sure that the pattern does not line up with the pattern of the previous section. You must rotate the stencil slightly and shift it up or down a small amount. This mismatch fools the eye into thinking that the pattern has a three-dimensional structure.

▷ As you complete each section, cover it up by replacing the freezer paper. Use Scotch tape to hold it in place. Open up the next section, and stencil, again making sure the pattern in each section is at a different angle and slightly offset from the pattern in adjacent sections.

▷ Continue until all sections have been stencilled (7).

▷ To stencil shadows, mask the towel with the taped-together sections of freezer paper. Put the big freezer-paper stencil, shown in Figure 2, back on the wall, only shift it down and over slightly to open up small gaps below the towel. Stencil the gaps with shadow glaze (8).

▷ Remove all freezer-paper pieces (9).

10

If you use a looser nongeometric pattern for the fabric, it can be harder to capture the pattern shift between folds. In this case, it helps to add some shading to the edges of each fold and to deepen the colors of the recessed folds (10).

Drapery and Curtains

Curtain and Swag Sketches

Before applying the basic drapery technique to applications bigger than a tea towel, you need to measure the size of the space you plan to fill and make scaled-down sketches for the shape you want the curtain or swag to take. Magazine photographs and pictures of murals are good sources of inspiration. I also find it helpful to use a brand-new flat sheet, still crisp with sizing, as a model. I swag it into the shapes I'm looking for and make pencil sketches. What you want to end up with is a line drawing in which the structure of the drape is defined by a number of mostly linear folds. Think of the fabric as highly starched, rather than soft and fluid. You want the folds to vary in size, shape and direction—nothing too repetitive.

Enlarge the line drawing, or pattern, to accommodate the size of your project, and transfer the pattern outline to the shiny side of a large piece of freezer paper (or other inexpensive stencil material). For very large projects, I tape sections of freezer paper together with clear packing tape to get the width I need.

As long as you stick with water-based paints, you can use a permanent felt pen to make the pattern outline. Occasionally, I find that even a permanent felt pen can cause slight discolorations in my stencilling. Test the pen first, and if this is a problem, use a very thin pen line and let it dry well before you start stencilling. The main thing is to stay away from water-soluble felt pens, because they will make a mess with your paints.

Draped Swag

When you have the time and some paint on hand but no money, this is one way to dress up a plain bedroom. The swag over this bed was a straight-forward application of the method just described on the previous five pages. I incorporated two types of faux fabric, making them intertwine across the swag. The green damask "fabric" was basecoated with a flat paint that matched the duvet cover. Its pattern was stencilled with a glossy latex paint in an almost identical color. It's mainly the difference in gloss between the basecoat and the stencilling that makes the pattern show up. Do you recognize the pattern? It's the same one I used on the china vase on page 64. It appears again, in different colors, on page 99.

The chintz "fabric" was basecoated in a pale toned-down yellow, and the rose pattern was added with a simple one-piece stencil and blended colors. Because this pattern was so loosely connected, I added stronger shading to each section of the swag.

Before removing the huge piece of taped-together freezer-paper sections, I stencilled the curtain rod and finials. By the way, the bed in this picture is a simple mattress and box-spring set—the headboard is also stencilled. The pattern for the headboard was drawn onto freezer paper with the aid of a dinner plate, a pie tin and a garden hose. The freezer paper was taped on the wall, where, one by one, each section was cut out, stencilled and covered up, until the whole thing was finished.

Drapery and Curtains

Lace Curtains

▷ This lace curtain was done the same way as the gingham one on page 94, with two main exceptions. First, you start with a night-sky background, created by brushing several layers of deep blue glaze and paint over a white background.

▷ Second, you basecoat the curtain section by section, instead of all at once, with a thin coat of white latex paint mixed with just enough clear acrylic glaze and extender to make it translucent and to give you about five minutes of open, or working, time. Apply this with a foam roller, building it up a little on the edges of the sections so that they look more opaque.

▷ Now wipe a cotton cloth or roll a dry foam roller down the middle of each section to remove some of the white. You want the center of the section to look fairly transparent and the long edges that define the folds to be more opaque (i.e., more white). Wherever the "fabric" should be bunched together, you also want to make opaque. If needed, brush a little more white paint on the parts you want more opaque.

▷ If you don't like the way it turns out, wipe it all off with a damp cloth, let the section dry and redo it. (Of course, you must decide right away that you don't like it; if you wait two hours, you won't be able to wipe it off.)

▷ When the basecoat is dry (speed up the process with a blow-dryer if you're impatient), stencil the lace pattern over the section, using opaque white.

▷ Repeat with each section.

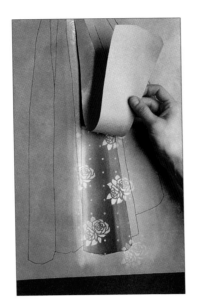

Windows With Curtains

Combining Curtain and Window

It's not a difficult step to combine a window stencil with the curtain technique, nor does it take much longer. Any extra time spent stencilling the curtain is offset by the time saved not having to stencil the parts of the window (and view) covered by the curtain.

There are three main steps. First, mark the position on the wall for the window-to-be, and decide where to position the curtain. Second, stencil the curtain, as described on pages 92 through 96, using a giant freezer-paper template. Third, mask the stencilled curtain, and stencil the window, including the sky and any view seen through the window. Here are the step-by-step instructions:

▷ As described on page 86, tape off the shape of your window and paint the whole thing white. When it's dry, trace the windowpane outlines using the stencil and a fine pencil.

▷ Transfer your curtain pattern to a large sheet of freezer paper, piecing together more than one sheet if necessary. I use clear packing tape for joining and am careful not to create any wrinkles at the join. Spray the back (the paper side) with stencil adhesive, and let dry.

▷ Cut out the entire curtain silhouette in one piece. Save the freezer paper that you cut away.

▷ Move the curtain silhouette into place over the window outline (1), and smooth out the wrinkles. Stand back, take a good look, and make sure that the curtain is positioned where you want it. Now take the other piece of freezer paper—the part that was cut off—and put it on the wall surrounding the curtain, making sure that the edges align perfectly (2). This is easier if you have a helper.

For a very large curtain, you may have to cut this surrounding piece into two sections for easier handling. Smooth it down so that the cut edges stick well, with no wrinkles. Just to be safe, use painters' tape to secure the outer edges.

▷ Remove the entire curtain silhouette, erase any visible pencil lines, and roller stencil the basecoat for the curtain (3). You may have to do more than one coat. Wait until it is thoroughly dry, then replace the curtain silhouette, taping in place.

▷ With a sharp craft knife, cut out one section, or fold, of the curtain (4).

▷ Stencil the fabric pattern over this exposed section (5). Position the freezer paper over the section just stencilled, and tape it in place. Cut out and stencil another section, as shown for the tea towel example (page 94). Continue until the entire curtain has been stencilled.

▷ Remove only the freezer paper surrounding the curtain sections; leave the taped-together pieces covering the curtain in place as a mask. Use painters' tape to keep the mask firmly in place. Position the window stencil over the curtain mask, lining it up carefully with the white rectangle and the pencil marks. Tape it in place. If there are a large number of windowpanes exposed, you can lay strips of one-inch painters' tape between the panes instead of using the stencil. This will save you having to move the stencil after every four panes.

▷ Follow the basic window instructions to stencil sky, plants and shadows (6). Stencil a curtain rod. Remove the remaining freezer paper.

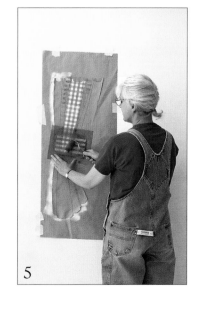

Windows With Curtains

Tartan Curtain on Woodgrain Door

Here is another hollow-core door project. For this large curtain, the tartan (shown in steps on page 93) was executed entirely with foam rollers. Because the curtain technique is so easy and the fabric so dramatic, I chose to cover most of the door and leave little room for the view, which often takes more effort.

Following the steps described on page 100, I started with the door painted flat white, used a stencil to outline the position of the windowpanes and made the freezer-paper template for the curtain. Once the template was in place, I stencilled a deep red basecoat for the entire curtain. I applied several thin coats and let them dry overnight. With the curtain mask in place, I cut out one section at a time and stencilled it with the tartan pattern: vertical black stripes and horizontal black stripes, followed by narrow yellow accent stripes. For all the large sections, I used a slightly curved stencil for the horizontal stripes to heighten the sense of realism.

When all the sections of the curtain had been stencilled, I removed the surrounding freezer paper and made sure that the large curtain mask was taped securely in place. Next, I positioned the window stencil and painted the sky, grass and rhododendrons.

Once the view was finished, I removed the window stencil and stuck freezer-paper masks over the exposed windowpanes. Then I painted the white door frame with a wood-colored glaze, through which I pulled a woodgraining tool. After the frames were woodgrained, I gave them stencilled highlights and shadows. Finally, I stencilled the curtain rod.

The last step was to remove the masks from the panes and lift off the large piece of freezer-paper sections masking the curtain (shown at left).

Windows With Curtains

Tropical Windows

This room has a long stretch of solid wall broken only by two tall and very narrow windows that let in a little light but no view. I've supplemented those windows with a set of fake ones of similar size and curtain treatment. I made the windows look recessed by painting shaded and highlighted bands of wall color next to the window frames. To emphasize the recess, I stencilled a small pot of geraniums on one of the windowsills.

The method used here is exactly the same as the one used in the previous examples: mark the window positions, stencil the curtains, stencil the windowpane views, stencil the shadows. I put a horizon in here because I wanted to make a tropical-ocean setting. All the palm trees are built from a single palm-frond stencil by making many overlapping prints and using different hues of green. Instead of being held up by traditional curtain rods, the curtains hang from stencilled pieces of driftwood.

The parrot keeps the setting from looking too static; it also covers up a piece of sky that I wasn't very happy with. The parrot was stencilled in three steps: one to lay down a base-coat of yellow with some jungle-green shading; the second to add the green feather detailing; and the third to do the black beak and red throat.

Inside/Outside Door

Just as the tartan door was woodgrained instead of left white, I've painted this door a rich navy blue, mainly because I wanted a color that would let the lace show up by contrast. This lace is different from the previous example; it's like a crocheted textile, with a very open weave, whereas the other one was more like a sheer, smooth-textured fabric. In fact, I used a real piece of lace as a stencil. The whimsical part about this door is the other side. It's been stencilled to resemble the outside of the door looking into the house.

Both the inside and the outside views of the door use the same stencils and masks: a window stencil, windowpane masks and a piece of lace that just covers the window when laid flat. The difference between the views lies in the order in which the stencils and masks are used. Before you begin, stretch the piece of lace flat and use a foam roller to coat it with shellac or latex paint. Let dry. This will stiffen the lace and make it easy to reposition, just like a normal stencil. Spray the underside generously with stencil adhesive, and let dry. You must also cut some windowpane masks out of freezer paper or Mylar, using the window stencil for a pattern.

◆ **Outside View**

▷ Put the window stencil in place. Lightly trace the outline of each pane with a fine pencil. Position the piece of stiffened lace on top of the window stencil (1). Smooth out any wrinkles, and press in place. Secure the edges with tape to ensure that the lace doesn't shift.
▷ Roller stencil taupe-colored latex paint through the lace, covering all panes in the window (2). Lift a corner of the lace to make sure the print is clear. If you haven't picked up sufficient detail, you may have to go over it a second time, pouncing the color with a large, stiff stencil brush.
▷ Remove the lace. Leave the window stencil in place.
▷ Pick up a small amount of shadow glaze on a large stencil brush, and rub a few soft vertical streaks over the lace print (3). The idea is to add a few hints of shadow so that the lace looks slightly undulating instead of flat.
▷ Remove the window stencil (4). Using the pencil outlines as a guide, mask each pane of the window with a Mylar or freezer-paper rectangle. Use stencil adhesive to hold the masks in place. With a foam roller, paint the entire door blue (5). When painting over the masks, use a minimum amount of paint (just as though you were stencilling) to keep the paint from seeping under the masks. This area will take several thin coats of blue to build up the right color.

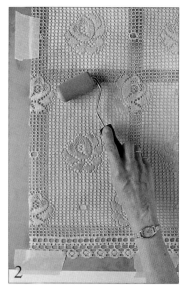

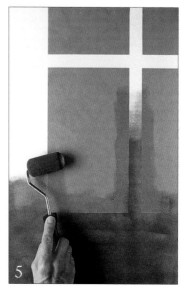

◆ Inside View

▷ Position the window stencil, and outline the panes in fine pencil. Remove the window stencil. Using the pencil lines as a guide, mask the panes with freezer-paper rectangles. Place the lace over the masked panes, lining up the lace edges more or less parallel to the edges of the door. Press down firmly so that the stencil adhesive gets a good grip. Roller stencil navy-blue latex paint over the entire lace surface (1), being careful not to let the lace shift (help anchor it with your spare hand). Lift a corner of the lace to check on the print. If there is insufficient detail, go over it again, stippling with a stiff stencil brush. Then continue to cover the rest of the door in blue as well.

▷ Remove the lace carefully (2, 3), and lay it aside, flat, for the moment. Try not to stretch it.

▷ Remove the freezer-paper masks (4).

▷ Using the pencil lines as a guide, position the window stencil (5). Replace the lace, laying it on top of the window stencil (6). Line up the lace pattern with the parts that were stencilled blue in the first step.

▷ Now you fill in the filtered outdoor "view" that's slightly visible through the lace. Roller stencil the top part of the window with a light sky blue, and do a small strip at the bottom with a light warm green (7). As before, lift a corner of the lace to check on the print. If there is insufficient detail, stipple over the lace with a stiff stencil brush.

▷ Remove the lace and the stencil (8). When the paint is completely dry, use a clean vinyl eraser to remove any visible pencil lines.

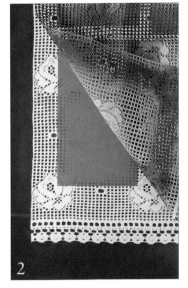

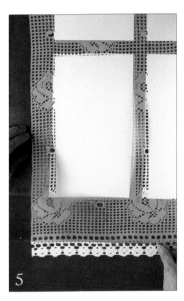

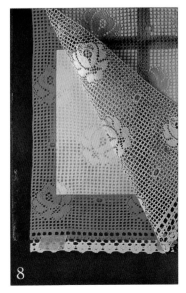

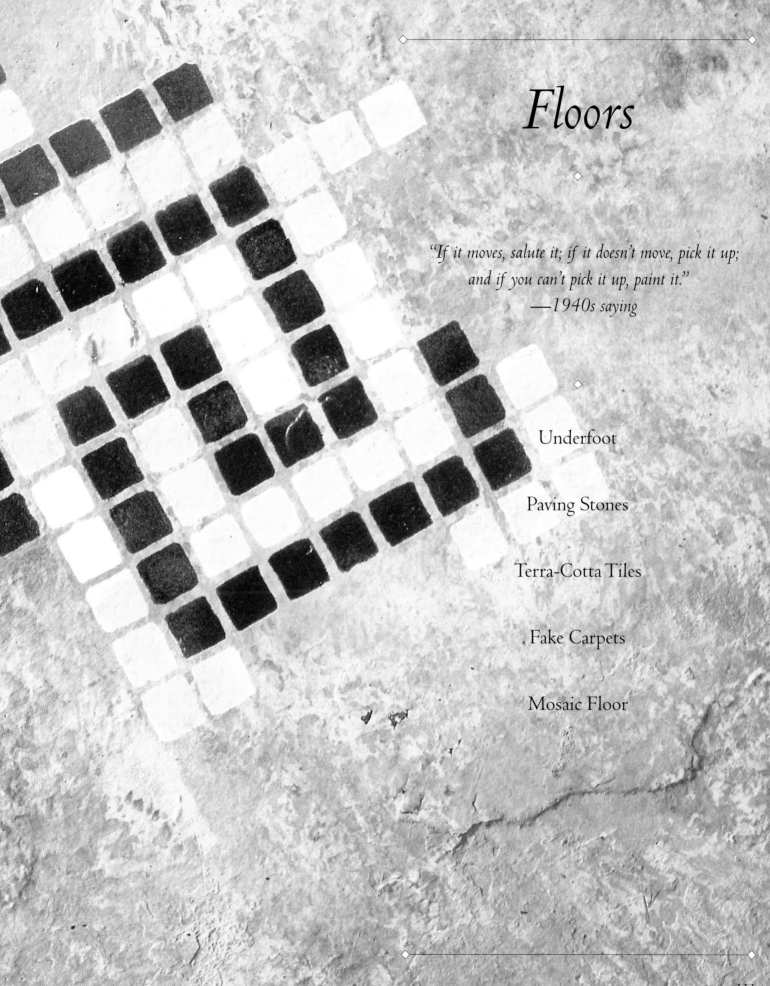

Floors

*"If it moves, salute it; if it doesn't move, pick it up;
and if you can't pick it up, paint it."*
—1940s saying

Underfoot

Paving Stones

Terra-Cotta Tiles

Fake Carpets

Mosaic Floor

For some time, I've avoided the major costs and hassles of refinishing our wood floors by painting fake carpets directly onto the worn spots. It's cheap, it's easy, and like the General Paint ad says, it lasts forever. The only problem is that visitors usually stop in their tracks when they reach one, as it suddenly occurs to them that this rug is painted, not woven. Unsure of whether it's socially acceptable to tread on a "painting," they generally end up walking around it, thus hastening the demise of the rest of the floor.

One of the first of many such "carpets" was a runner intended to obscure damage inflicted along the shortest route between our front-yard "soccer field" and the kitchen fridge, a route that passes along the eastern edge of the living room. Using latex paint and stencil rollers, I stencilled the basecoat with endless rows of a zigzag Navajo pattern, then sealed the whole thing with three coats of acrylic varnish. It's virtually indestructible.

Both my sister and I have also had great luck renovating linoleum floors with paint. We basecoat, then stencil fake tiles over the entire surface. With four coats of acrylic varnish on top, the "new" floors hold up wonderfully to family traffic, pets and parties. Top up the varnish every year or so, and it lasts a long time. It saves a lot of money when the alternative is investing in all-new linoleum. Concrete and timeworn wood floors are also ideal candidates for paint treatments.

As always, the most important step is also the most tedious: preparing the surface for the first coat of paint. If you skip this step, you risk losing your decorative treatment chip by chip. First, make sure the floor is clean and grease-free. Strip off any wax, and scrape away any loose paint. Thoroughly rinse off any cleaner. Rough up the surface with some sandpaper to give it enough tooth to hold the paint.

Ask your paint dealer to recommend a paint for your basecoat. It's not necessary to use an oil-based or alkyd paint. My sister used an acrylic porch paint, and I used an acrylic reported to have excellent adhesion to glossy surfaces. Don't use anything shinier than an eggshell finish, because you still need to stencil over it. The final coats of protective acrylic varnish will provide whatever gloss you want.

Unless you're working in a vacant house or apartment, your biggest challenges will be isolating your work so that the family can still get to the fridge and keeping the dog hairs at bay until the varnish has dried. My sister's "tile" floor was easier than mine because her cat is smart enough to stay away from wet paint, whereas our springer spaniel…Well, need I say more? They aren't called springers for nothing.

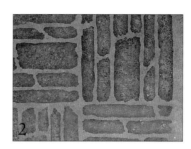

This is a good treatment for a beat-up old floor, especially in a child's room or any room with a garden theme. Here are two variations on a stone floor: the first with blocks of rough-cut rock and the second with smoother, round cobblestones.

◆**Rough-Cut Rock Floor**
The first example uses the same stencil as the rock wall on page 74. A heat cutter is great for a stencil like this, because it lets you put random wobbles in the cuts very easily.
▷ Paint the floor with the color of your "grout." Here, I wanted it to be rather rough, so I started with a medium brown basecoat, then added random drifts of moss green, black and taupe with a large sea sponge. Before the sponged paint dried completely, I rolled a dry foam roller over it to do some rough blending.
▷ When the painted grouting is dry, position your rock stencil and roller stencil a rock basecoat (I used a taupe color for this). With the stencil still in place, sponge on drifts of white and black. As with the grouting basecoat, run a dry foam roller over the sponged paint.
▷ Before removing the stencil, lift one corner to make sure there is enough contrast between the edges of the rocks and the grouting (1).
▷ To keep the floor from looking as though it has been stamped with 150 identical repeats, rotate every other set of prints through 90 degrees, like a parquet flooring (2).
▷ To give the rocks more definition, you need to add some shadows (3, 4). Mix a little brown or black paint into some shadow glaze (it must be less transparent to show up over these stones). Use a round

artist's brush to paint a strip of this mix along the shadowed edges of each rock (3), allowing it to overlap about a quarter-inch of "rock" and a quarter-inch of "grout."

▷ You can also imply cracks or striations in the rock by painting meandering lines with the glaze mixture (5).

◆ **Cobblestone Floor**

The pattern for the second stone floor is based on a mold for making concrete cobblestones, sold by my favorite tool company, Lee Valley. Each cast of the mold makes a block of nine cobblestones, shaped so that when you do an adjacent block, you rotate the mold to get an interlocking fit with the first block. Because of the rotation, it's impossible to recognize the repeat pattern.

▷ Paint and sponge the floor in grout colors, here mostly browns, with some mossy green in places. Let it dry.

▷ Position your rock stencil, and roller stencil a rock basecoat (here, it's taupe), adding patches and streaks of slightly different hues.

▷ To give the cobblestones a little more realism, you need to shade the edges. Outline each stencilled stone with a soft (2B) lead pencil. Take a small stencil brush with short, stiff bristles, pick up a little shadow glaze (with or without paint added, depending on how subtle an effect you want), and rub the brush firmly along the pencil lines. The pencil lines will darken as soon as they get wet and will smudge as you rub them. Smudges of color will fade out from the pencil lines onto the edges of the stone (giving the stones the illusion of height) and also onto the space between the stones.

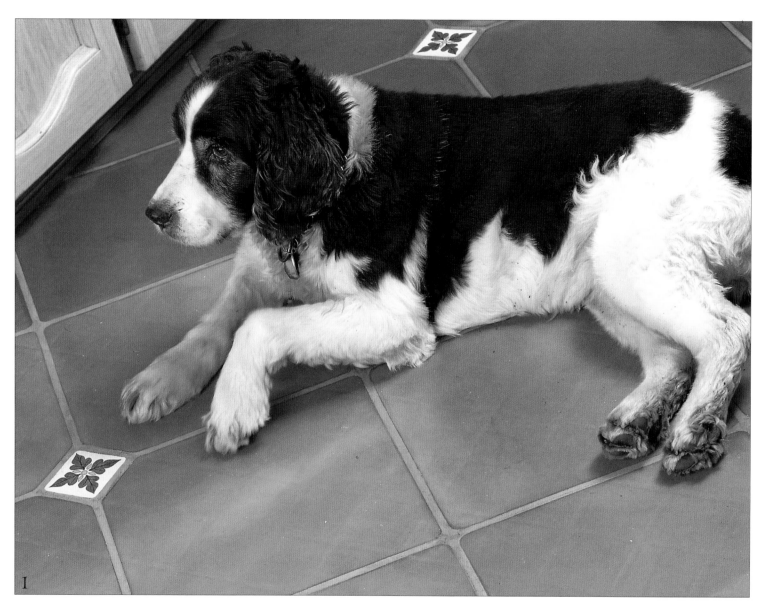

These "tiles" have been stencilled over linoleum that was way past its prime. After stripping, cleaning, scuffing, et cetera, you start by painting the floor grout-gray.

▷ Stencil the terra-cotta tiles with foam stencil rollers and latex acrylic paint in roughly blended colors of terra-cotta and ocher (1). To build up the depth of color you need, stencil the tiles a second time once the first coat has thoroughly dried. Repositioning the tile stencil for the second coat will be faster if you keep your stencil oriented the same way for all the tiles when you do the first coat.

▷ For a little extra interest, you can insert small colored or patterned tiles between the corners of the big tiles. Stencil these small squares with opaque white (2). When thoroughly dry, stencil over them a second time to make the white brighter.

▷ Stencil the green and yellow motif in the center of each white tile.

▷ Outline each part of the motif with a liner squeeze bottle filled with acrylic paint (3, 4).

▷ How dirty you want your grouting to look is a matter of choice. Most of us would prefer a real tile floor to be clean, but there is no question that a little faux dirt makes a painted floor look more realistic. Here's one way of getting some into the grouting. Outline each tile with a dark brown watercolor pencil. Prepare a thin mixture of shadow glaze and water. Load a liner brush with a generous amount of this mixture, and outline the tiles again, covering the pencil lines and letting the glaze overlap both the tile edge and the grout (5). Always brush in the direction of the tile edge, and don't overwork it. The pencil lines should dissolve, leaving a fine but slightly diffuse dark line where the tile and grout meet. The glaze makes the edge of the tile look somewhat rounded and the grout slightly dirty (6). For comparison, check the two floors on the facing page. One has been given this treatment around the terra-cotta tiles but not around the white tiles (1). The other has no "dirt" at all (2). On this latter floor, the linoleum that was painted over had an embossed surface in the shape of simulated tiles. The stencilled tiles were created to match the size and shape of the embossed ones, giving a three-dimensional reinforcement to the illusion.

▷ Let the floor dry for one or two days, then give it at least four coats of acrylic varnish, following the instructions on the label. Don't walk on the floor for a day or two, then walk only in stocking feet for a week while the varnish cures.

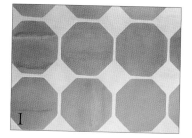

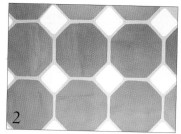

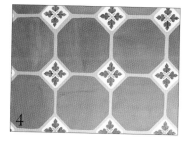

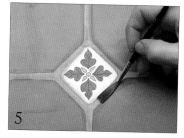

Fake Carpets

Tone on Tone

I've been using painted "rugs" to cover up worn spots on the floor for years. When I want something quick and easy, I pick Southwestern or Navajo geometric designs, because they lend themselves so well to stencils and can be beautifully executed with latex paints and foam stencil rollers.

This rug, shown in full on page 119, is an example of background stencilling, using single overlay stencils. The design is derived from an old Peruvian tapestry. The following instructions illustrate the method used for part of the border pattern, shown here in tone-on-tone colors.

I find that large, intricate but not particularly precise stencils like this are best attempted with a heat cutter, a glass of wine and a Bryn Terfel CD, or maybe Patsy Cline, depending on the mood of the moment. If you're not in a rush, the stencil will practically cut itself.

The easiest way to stencil this design is using only two colors.
▷ Use strips of painters' tape to mask off the shape of the carpet.
▷ Make sure that the area bounded by the tape is clean and has enough tooth to bond to paint. Sand lightly if necessary. If you get down to bare wood, you will need to apply a primer.
▷ Paint a basecoat with latex paint in the lighter of your two chosen colors. Here, I've used a light taupe. When dry, apply a second coat. To avoid brush marks, I used a foam roller for these steps.
▷ To make the carpet look more interesting, divide it into a center section that you can stencil with one pattern and a border section with a different pattern. Only the border pattern is shown here.
▷ Position the border stencil, and use a roller method to cover the stencil cutouts evenly with the darker of your two colors (1). The result gives you a light pattern on a slightly darker background (2).

Fake Carpets

Multicolored

1

2

3

4

5

The same carpet stencils can be used to produce a completely different effect when multiple colors are used, as shown in the example opposite.

▷ The preparatory steps are the same as for the tone-on-tone carpet, except you start with a white basecoat so that the colors will glow. The center section of this carpet is then taped and painted red. The black pattern is stencilled over the red.

▷ The border section begins as solid green, with blocks of red and gold. Then the stencil is printed, entirely in black, on top of these colors to produce the black background. To start the border, you need to know where to put your patches of color. You do this by making a light print of the background stencil using a roller method (1).

▷ Block in patches of red wherever the lilylike flowers appear (2).

▷ Tape the edges of the border, then use a foam roller to cover everything that's not red with green latex paint, painting right over the black (3). This step is easier if you mask off your red patches. The green doesn't have to be perfectly even or opaque. You will still be able to see the black showing through.

▷ Put the border stencil back in place, and roller stencil the whole thing with black latex paint (4). The black may not seem to be covering very well, but if you check under the stencil, it will appear substantially more solid (5).

▷ Add a fringe to the carpet with a stencil or, as shown on the facing page, with a liner bottle and black latex paint.

Mosaic Floor

This fake mosaic look is an easy way to add interest to a floor or tabletop. It's especially effective on concrete surfaces. There are two ways of constructing a mosaic design. The easiest way (the one used here) is to work with a regular grid, in which all the tiles are the same size and shape. Any pattern is created by changing the colors of certain tiles. The second method has tiles of different sizes, shapes and colors. It can be used to devise much more sophisticated images, but because of the variety of the tile shapes, any stencilled copy involves a great deal of stencil cutting.

In this example, I've made the floor look more worn (and decreased the amount of work involved) by leaving out random patches of tile, as though they had become dislodged and swept away over the years.

▷ Start by rolling or sponging a mottled-gray basecoat. This will be the grout. It should be a color that will contrast nicely with the color of the tiles.

▷ The main stencil is a simple grid of square tile shapes with slightly rounded corners. I used a heat knife to cut this stencil so that I could make the tile edges and corners a little less than perfect.

▷ Tape the grid stencil over the basecoat so that there is no danger of its shifting (it has to stay in place for several steps).

▷ Roller stencil this grid with the color that accounts for most of the tiles (1). In this example, it is a light yellow ocher of inconsistent hue. Each time I reloaded the foam roller, I altered the color slightly to keep everything from getting too uniform.

▷ Because stencilling deposits such a thin film of paint, you must use two coats with this stencil. The first coat should be more than touch-dry before you add the second, so give it a few seconds' blow with a hair dryer.

▷ Leave the grid stencil in place, and on top of it, lay a second stencil, cut to reveal any tiles that will be given a different color. In this case, I wanted to create a narrow black border and a black fret pattern. The overlay exposes the tiles you want to turn black and masks off everything else. Overlay cutouts should be slightly generous so that exposed tiles are completely exposed. Any bridges must be narrower than the bridges on the grid stencil. With a foam roller, stencil the overlay with black latex or acrylic paint (2).

▷ Remove both stencils (3). Position the grid stencil for the next set of ocher tiles, and repeat the procedure. To create missing tiles, simply stick tape over parts of the grid stencil.

▷ The center part of my mosaic floor was filled in quickly with just the grid stencil and no overlay, except for a few black accent tiles here and there.

▷ The grid stencil can be used as the basis for any number of mosaic designs, on its own for plain sections and together with an overlay for patterned sections.

Stone & Shadow

◆

"Tell a man there are 300 billion stars in the universe,
and he'll believe you.
Tell him a bench has wet paint on it,
and he'll have to touch it to be sure."
—Anonymous

◆

Seeing Is Believing

Basic Stone Technique

Fireplace Screen With Stone Urn

Stone Terrace

Stone Balustrades

Columns and Dentil Border

Faux Fireplace

Garden Wall

I assured my publisher and his staff that my balustrade was nothing but paint, but they didn't believe it.

For months, designer Linda Menyes and I had been working on cover ideas for *Stencilling on a Grand Scale*. After reviewing and rejecting a score of possible projects, we finally created one from scratch that featured most of the important topics addressed in this book. The finished panel was eight feet long, conceived so that the balustrade, once photographed, would wrap around the front and back of the book cover. With the exception of the two- and three-inch honeysuckle blossoms (the project's most complicated stencil), the whole panel called for only three one-piece stencils, the largest of which was the size of a single baluster. We thought it perfectly illustrated just how far you can go with a few simple stencils.

"It looks too real," came the response. When the sales reps looked at the print of the proposed cover, they weren't able to figure out exactly what had been stencilled. Everyone thought it was a photograph of an actual balustrade. As Lewis Carroll wrote in *Through the Looking Glass,* "It's large as life and twice as natural."

Stencilling great stone is easier than it looks. The first step is to stencil the entire silhouette with a paint treatment that simulates some kind of stone. The second step is to make the silhouette three-dimensional by stencilling shadows, either by rubbing transparent color along the edge of a straight-edged mask or by using an overlay stencil. The texture and variations of the stone show through the stencilled shadows, creating a very realistic effect with little effort on your part. The straight-edge method of shadow shaping is demonstrated opposite using a baluster stencil.

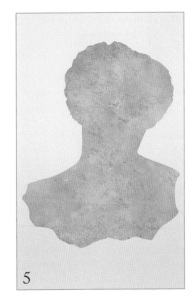

1

2

3

4

5

6

◆ Basic Stone

▷ Using a combination of sponging and rolling, fill in an overall silhouette stencil with broken colors (1). Here, I have used taupe, black and white.

▷ Run a brayer (a hard rubber roller used in printmaking) or a dry foam roller over the whole thing (with the stencil still in place) to disguise the sponged texture and do a rough blending of the colors (2). It will also pick up some irregular patches of paint, making the stone look weathered. Before continuing, let paint dry completely to ensure that the stone effect is not compromised.

▷ Use a large stencil brush and some shadow glaze (with or without added pigment) to shade the edges of the silhouette, simulating roundness.

◆ Straight-Edge Shadow Shaping

▷ Use a small stencil brush and some shadow glaze tinted with extra black to carve shapes and crevices with simulated shadows. You do this by laying a piece of painters' tape or Mylar horizontally across the stencil wherever you want to shape, say, a crevice. Draw a

thin pencil line along the tape. Now brush your dark glaze along the tape, on top of the pencil line (3). Your brush should be almost dry, just as though you were making a normal stencil print. The pencil line will smudge a little; it marks the deepest part of the crevice. The glaze will taper off as it gets farther from the crevice.

▷ Although the glaze has color, it is still transparent, so the texture of the stone shows through. The effect is almost magic, as the shadows cause shapes to emerge from the flat stone texture (4).

◆ Overlay Shadow Shaping

▷ Shaping shadows can also be done using overlay stencils, as shown with this garden statue.

▷ Stencil the silhouette, using the previous stone "recipe" or one of your choice (5). Shade the right side with shadow glaze, and highlight the left side with a little white glaze.

▷ Apply shadow glaze through the single overlay stencil (6). Pick up a little dark paint with the glaze when you stencil the right-hand side, which is in shadow.

You can apply these techniques using a number of

fake stone or marble recipes. Remember that as long as you are using a stencil, you must apply the paint or glaze carefully and sparingly near the stencil edges, or you risk bleeding the color under the edges. In the middle of the stencil or anywhere away from the edges, you can do what you want with the paint. The shapes you create may be a combination of shadows and highlights; it all depends on where the light is coming from. Highlights are stencilled the same way as the shadows, using lighter glazes.

A dark stone urn and strong, somber colors go a long way toward making a floral composition look moody and almost masculine. A fireplace screen like this one is an ideal project on which to practice. The frame and panel are both easily made of medium-density fiberboard (MDF). The stencilling is easier if you work on the individual pieces before putting them together.

▷ For this screen, I basecoated the panel, then covered it unevenly with a tinted plaster compound. When it was dry, I sanded it until parts of the basecoat showed through and the surface was smooth.

▷ After pencilling in the position of the urn, I stencilled the flower grouping. Then I cut a mask to cover the leaves that overhang the urn and stencilled the urn, using the stone technique described on the previous page. I made the texture look quite smooth by sponging very finely and by using a dry roller to smooth out the flecks.

▷ I left the urn stencil in place and let the paint dry. Using a large stencil brush, I blended a dark glaze around the edges to give the urn some roundness. Then, wherever I wanted a ridge or crevice, I laid a straight strip of Mylar across the stencil and ran a small stencil brush (with dark shadow glaze) along it to create tapered shadows.

Stone Terrace

While a scene like this one looks impressive, it has a couple of attributes that make it quite easy. First, there is no perspective, and all the shadows are linear. Except for the base of the columns, all the stencil cuts are straight lines. The angles are either 45 or 90 degrees, so it's easy to lay out the pattern on grid paper or on a computer screen and really easy to enlarge, even without a photocopier.

The sky might be difficult if you had to do an entire wall at one go, but the columns serve to break the sky up into manageable panels. You can easily do each panel of sky without getting lap lines.

▷ Start with the sky. With a strip of painters' tape marking off the horizon, use a brush or roller to fill in the entire upper area between columns. I used a mixture of acrylic glaze and blue latex paint for most of the sky, then blended in white and burnt umber to create clouds. For a more impressionistic approach to the sky, you could use a wash of latex paint, water and extender, brushed on loosely over a white background. Or, if you need something that absolutely cannot go wrong, you could go with a plain solid coat of blue paint.

▷ When the sky is thoroughly dry, move the tape on the horizon so that it masks the sky side of the horizon line. Now paint the water below the sky. Use an ordinary brush for this, applying the paint in short, horizontal strokes, without too much blending. Make the color deeper at the horizon and sufficiently different from the sky that the horizon is clearly evident. Throw in some hori-

zontal highlights of white or
lighter blue toward the lower
edge of the water. Don't worry
if it looks less than great at this
point. Once that vast expanse
of water gets broken up by the
stonework, it will look fine.

▷ Measure and mark the
placement of the balustrade.
Run long strips of low-tack
painters' tape along the edges
of the horizontal railings (upper and lower). Use the basic
stone technique described on
page 125 to fill in the railings.
Before removing the tape, highlight the upper edge and shade
the lower edge of the railing by
rubbing shadow glaze along
the edges with a stencil brush.
Make one or more recessed
edges under the hand railing
with the straight-edge shadow
technique described on page
125. Lay down a straight edge
of Mylar or painters' tape
parallel to the lower edge of
the railing. Pick up a small
amount of shadow glaze
(mixed with a bit of black)
on a stencil brush, and rub it
along the edge of the Mylar.
Continue until the entire length
of the railing has been shaded.

▷ Tape and paint straight
pillars in the same way as the
railings. Shade the edges of
the pillars with shadow glaze
using a foam roller. Stencil and
shade bases for the pillars.

▷ The stencil for the sections
of the balustrade looks like
half of the letter X, as outlined
in the close-up on this page.
(You could get faster coverage
with a stencil twice as large in
the shape of an entire letter X,
but I found this size was too
unwieldy.) Fit the stencil in
place between upper and lower
horizontal rails, and paint it
with the same stone technique.

▷ Move the stencil over to fill

in the other sections of the
balustrade. You have to rotate
the stencil for every other section in order to get the second
half of the X shape.

▷ The shadows and highlights
are done with shadow glaze
and a white-tinted glaze.
Both use the same stencil,
whose outline is shown in the
close-up photograph. This
stencil, with its diagonal stripes
and mitered corners, fills in
multiple shadows (or highlights) for one edge at a time.
It needs to be rotated appropriately for the other edges.

Stone Balustrades

Balustrades make particularly handy motifs for the aspiring muralist because they let you cover the length of a wall very effectively without requiring a huge talent. They look good on their own over a plain wall or even better over a simple glazed finish. You don't really need to add anything else.

If you want to go further, you can create almost any kind of scene around the balustrade or alter its mood with a different choice of stone color. Design an entire garden, or just add a few vines. Paint a distant landscape, or simply opt for fog. You can even adapt it for a child's room by stencilling animals or fairy-tale characters romping through the balusters. Because the stonework looks finished on its own, you can take your time with any embellishments. Add a few parrots now, and wait until next year to tackle the jungle. In the meantime, no one will realize you've only finished half the plan.

These balustrades were done using the basic stone technique already described. The railings were filled in and shaded first between lengths of low-tack tape. Then the balusters were stencilled, one at a time, with a single silhouette template and shaped with shading as illustrated on page 125. For the example on this page, I used a simple honeysuckle border stencil to start the plant winding out of the urn, then switched to small stencils of individual leaves and blossoms to make it thick and lush.

The folding screen combines stone and shadow stencilling with the fake-fabric technique described in "Drapery and Curtains" (page 92).

Columns and Dentil Border

If you're not up to the effort involved in painting fake marble or granite for your stonework, you can opt for plain white, as I did for these columns and the dentil border.

The first step was to paint the simulated crown molding. I painted a white strip at the top of the walls. The shadows that shape the dentil molding were roller stencilled on top of this strip in a light taupe latex paint. Small bits of darker shading were picked out with a ½-inch stencil brush in between the "teeth" of the molding.

The top part of the column (called a capital) was roller stencilled in three steps: the basic silhouette in white, the first overlay of light shadows in a very light taupe and the second overlay in a darker taupe. Some extra shading was added with a brush.

I made sure that the column base was positioned directly below the capital. It was roller stencilled in two steps, with shading added by brush.

To create the white base-coat for the shaft of the column, I stretched two strips of painters' tape between the capital and the base and filled the area with two coats of white latex paint, applied with a foam roller.

An overlay provided the template for the carved flutes. I ran a light pencil line down the left-hand edge of each flute cutout (the light was coming from the top left), then stencilled the flutes with a light touch of shadow glaze. I used a small stencil brush to add extra shading to the top and left-hand edges of each flute, making sure that the pencil lines were blended into the shadows.

Faux Fireplace

Can't afford a real fireplace? Or maybe you live in a condo where it's just not possible. Then get out your stencil stuff, and create a fake fireplace on a panel, on a flat cabinet or on the wall, like this one. Add some stencilled pewter candlesticks on the mantel. And to give it an air of legitimacy, hang a real painting or mirror above it and put a real fireplace screen in front of it—decorated with stencils, of course.

First, you need to decide on a shape for your fireplace. Most libraries have one or two books on fireplaces in their home-decorating sections, and this is a good place to start. I made mine up from a combination of sources, because I had quite a few constraints. I chose a classical shape mostly defined by straight edges so that I could use strips of tape to achieve its silhouette, rather than cutting an elaborate stencil. This also meant that I could use the straight-edge method of shading to bring out most of the fireplace contours.

Finally, I was able to fit my dentil-molding stencil under the mantel, which left only one small stencil to cut—that of the Victorian honeysuckle motif.

I began by taping the outline of the entire fireplace and filling it in with a quick marble treatment:

▷ Gray and white latex paint, rolled and sponged in large drifts, then blended with a large, soft brush.

▷ Several layers of veins applied with a feather and blended.

▷ A final top layer of very thin veins applied with a watercolor pencil crayon, misted *very* lightly with water, then blended with a soft touch.

The next step was to measure and draw light pencil lines outlining each section of the fireplace (i.e., mantelpiece, the ridges under the mantel, the corner pieces, and so on). Each of these sections was given definition by shading the edges with shadow glaze, keeping everything transparent so that the marble veining showed through the shadows. The dentil molding was stencilled in shadow glaze, as was the honeysuckle motif. Finally, the firebox was filled in completely with several layers of a dark acrylic glaze/latex paint mix, applied with a foam roller.

The candlesticks were done in two steps using a single stencil. First, the silhouette was stencilled in gray and silver. Then, with the silhouette stencil still in place, dark shading was added to bring out details of the shape, in the same way that the stone balusters were contoured.

Garden Wall

Ever since I saw the movie *Green Card*, I've wanted a little conservatory. Filtered sunlight, exotic plants, the lush scent of earth and moss and, especially, the trickle of water into a little stone basin set against the wall. Well, my conservatory is not likely to materialize unless I win a lottery. In the meantime, I'll just feed my daydreams with an indoor garden wall made from a few dollars' worth of paint and some elbow grease.

This is just another application of the basic stone technique: First, the entire area was covered with a paint treatment that simulates stone (here, I used yellow ocher, white and warm browns). Then shadow glazes and highlights were used with one or more stencil overlays to shape the bricks, the lion's head and the basin. As before, thin pencil lines sharpened the deep shadow edges.

The lion was particularly easy, with only two stencils: one for a light shadow glaze, the other for a darker glaze. Again, the glazes provide transparent color, so the stone texture shows through. Three overlays were used for the shell-shaped basin, and the stream of water was painted freehand using a small, round artist's brush and white paint mixed with clear glaze.

It's not necessary to stencil bricks over an entire wall. You can "brick" just a small section and leave the rest of the wall with a flat-stone treatment.

Frankly Fake

◇

"You can fool too many of the people too much of the time."
—James Thurber

◇

Quick, Easy and Removable

Bed Corner

Balustrade and Potted Palms

Folding Screen

I could stencil Genghis Khan and his mighty hordes charging over the bathtub, and my husband wouldn't notice. How do I know? I extrapolate from past experience. Once, when he was off on a month-long trip to Tasmania, I painted the white bathroom navy blue, covered the walls with white stencilled tulips, installed wainscoting and replaced the sink, vanity and flooring. On his return, his only reaction was to call out from the shower, "Hey, we're out of shampoo!"

Most spouses, though, often seem to have one big thing in common with landlords and real estate agents: they like their walls off-white and unadorned. Organize a stencil class, and you'll see what I mean. At least one frustrated painter will admit that her stencilling never touches a wall because her spouse and/or landlord won't permit it or because her spouse and/or real estate agent says that it will decrease the resale value.

Short of leaving your spouse or changing landlords, there are a few alternatives. You can stencil a movable camouflage, such as a folding screen or hanging panels, that can be packed up with the sofa when you move. Or you can just accept the fact that at some point, you will have to paint out your work with a few coats of solid off-white. If you have duplicated the Sistine Chapel on your ceiling, you might find this hard to do, but if the painted decoration was quick and easy to start with, it's not so painful to get rid of it. Sometimes, quick and easy just makes more sense than slow and laborious.

I'm used to short-lived wall decoration, because our house is also my studio, and its walls are my work surface. The paint effect on any given wall sometimes lasts only as long as is needed for a photo shoot. The northwest corner of the dining room might be temporarily stencilled as a nursery, while the southeast corner stands in for a pantry. The shortest-lived mural I ever did was a large tree that covered a bedroom wall. I was still stencilling it while the photographer was setting up, and as soon as he got his shot, I picked up a roller and started painting it out.

Quick and easy doesn't mean you have to forgo the impression of a big mural. It just means simplifying. You want to be able to stick up a stencil, paint it and be done with it. No messing with freeform or overlays or shadows. With this method, however, if you want a big picture, you do need a big stencil. Three easy approaches to big one-piece stencils are shown on the following pages.

A good example of movable decoration, this large canvas hangs from a painted wooden dowel (less expensive than a curtain rod) embellished with curtain-rod finials. Here, it acts as a headboard, but if the bed were backed into the corner of a room on the diagonal, it could also serve as a room divider, setting up space for storage or a dressing room behind. A canvas like this is very light and could easily be suspended from the ceiling by monofilament without leaving a noticeable trace for the landlord.

Start with a piece of pre-primed canvas, available by the yard from most art-supply stores. (It costs slightly more than unprimed canvas, but it's worth it, especially if you need a really large piece.) For the background, I used latex paints in creamy off-white and several greens, one of which matched the duvet cover. I applied them in drifts with a thin fabric roller, one color after another, roughly blending them wet into wet with the roller. When the surface was almost dry, I blended it again by rolling a brayer (a hard rubber roller used in printmaking) over it, which also removed random patches of paint, contributing to the effect of broken color. You can get a similar effect by using a dry foam roller.

This whole panel was done with large one-piece stencils. I spread the Mylar on a large table and cut out the stencils with a hardware-store utility knife—one stencil for the bouquet, another for the column. (Utility knives stay sharp longer than the finer X-acto knives and are great if you don't need fine precision.) There's no point in spending a lot on a stencil that you might use only once, so consider using freezer paper for this one.

Stencil adhesive is really helpful when working with big stencils like these, because it helps keep those long bridges from shifting. You must use painters' tape as well, because if the stencil falls off the wall, it will be really difficult to get it back in place. You could also lay the canvas flat on the floor for stencilling so that there's no risk of gravity causing the stencil to sag.

The only way to make a one-piece stencil like this look interesting is to use many colors and let them drift across bridges. I stencilled everything with foam rollers first and used brushes only to add a few accents of localized color.

While you are painting, keep checking under the stencil to preview the colors, because once you lift the whole thing, you don't want to have to try to put it back.

When it's all finished, attach the canvas to a long, painted dowel with short nails or staples.

This is an example of a temporary mural that goes right on the wall, and it is one that you might not mind painting out when the time comes, because it doesn't take a lot of effort —just a few easy one-piece stencils: one for the potted palm, another for a section of the balustrade.

Simple stencilling like this can be enhanced with some variability in the background. Here, I did what I call a soft parchment finish on the wall before starting. This finish is quick and easy and gives the wall a subtle look of broken color. Paint the basecoat, and let it dry overnight. Then, mix equal parts latex paint, acrylic glaze and water, and apply this over the basecoat with a foam roller, using random strokes and aiming for an uneven finish. For a slightly smoother effect, blend each section with a clean paintbrush before it dries. For a more complex finish, apply a second layer of glaze mixture over the first, using a different color.

The stone treatment used here is simpler than that in "Stone & Shadow" (page 123). There's no attempt at reality, because the bridges in the stencil print already tell you it's not meant to be real. All the colors are rather subdued to keep the obviously fake stencilled structures from leaping out of the wall. I used a large sea sponge to pounce drifts of white and taupe, with a touch of black, through the balustrade stencil and left it at that, with no shading. The small palms were roller stencilled in green.

Folding Screen

Folding screens, made from plywood, medium-density fiberboard (MDF) or bifolds, make good decorative room dividers. You can also spread them out flat against a wall to provide easily movable wall decoration. There are several examples of elaborately stencilled folding screens earlier in the book. Here's a simpler one. It employs a single large template for a Greek runner. The design is based on figures decorating a Panathenic amphora.

Instead of using bridges and colors to provide visual interest, as did the two previous examples, or overlays and shading to simulate reality, this silhouette stencil is simply used repeatedly to make identical overlapping prints. Really simple stencils like this usually look better when they are applied over some kind of faux finish or paint treatment.

These panels were first given a "Venetian plaster" finish (see Sources), for which a special tinted acrylic paste is applied in layers with a metal spatula, then burnished to a high sheen. Based on European polished plaster and cement treatments, this finish gives the impression of shifts in depth and color yet is smooth and cool to the touch.

Each runner was roller stencilled with a single color, but that color was modulated by being sanded back in places to the plaster background.

For a stencil like this, with no bridges to help keep its shape, you should consider using a rigid material such as stencil card. A commercial fret stencil was used to add the Greek borders.

Sources

Stencilling and Painting Materials

Stencilling has become so popular that stencils and accessory products are now widely available at most craft stores, paint and home-decorating centers, even some hardware stores. There are too many stencil companies to list here, but you can discover most of them, including their mail-order addresses, through the Stencil Artisans League, Inc., known as SALI for short. This is an international non-profit organization dedicated to the promotion and preservation of the art of stencilling and related decorative painting. Membership (not expensive) is open to amateurs, hobbyists and professionals alike and comes with a subscription to the quarterly magazine *The Artistic Stenciler*. SALI also hosts an annual convention, complete with classes and trade show.

Stencil Artisans League, Inc.
10521 Saint Charles Rock Road
Suite One
Saint Ann, Missouri
63074-1838
E-mail: SALISTL@aol.com

Venetian plaster classes and supplies are available through:

Ritins Studio Workshops
170 Wicksteed Avenue
Toronto, Ontario
Canada M4G 2B6

The projects in this book were executed almost entirely with Buckingham Stencils products. Most stencilling, whether by brush or by roller, was done with Buckingham Roller Stencil Paint. Acrylic craft paints were used to alter some hues, and Buckingham Blending Glaze was added wherever soft blending was needed. Background wall painting and faux finishes were done with General Paint and Benjamin Moore products, along with Symphony Faux & Decorative Glazes. The Venetian plaster treatment was done with Gothic Coatings' Marbleizer from Ritins Studio Workshops. Flecto Varathane Diamond Finish (acrylic varnish) was used to finish all floor projects. I used two brands of low-tack tape. For masking the ribs between the windowpanes of large windows, I used Kleen Edge®, because it comes in a width that is exactly one inch. For everything else (masking, registration marking and holding large stencils in place), I used Painters Mate® Delicate (it's pale green), because it is somewhat translucent and has no printing on it to interfere with my own markings. It is sold in various metric widths. I used Buckingham Stencils stencil adhesive spray to hold masks in place and to anchor stencils to the wall (I used tape as backup for large stencils). The small stool on page 51 was decorated using Cutbill Blocking™ block printing pads and glazes.

Many of the designs used in this book are available as commercial laser-cut stencils under the Buckingham Stencils label. They are manufactured and distributed by:

VeraDeco International Inc.
3430 South Service Road
Burlington, Ontario
Canada L7N 3T9
tel: 905-681-2318
or 1-800-742-8168
fax: 905-681-8485

Other Buckingham Stencils products manufactured by VeraDeco include roller paints, stencil rollers, stencil brushes, palettes, blending glaze, repositionable spray glue and an instructional video.

Retail mail-order service for Buckingham Stencils products is also available through:

Mary Maxim
tel: 888-442-2266 (for Canada only)
fax: 519-442-4520

The commercial stencils used in this book are listed at right. All other stencils were designed and hand-cut expressly for the projects in this book. They are not currently available as commercial stencils but may become so at some future date. For those readers who prefer to cut their own stencils, this book has many illustrations from which you can make stencil patterns for your own limited use.

◆ **Buckingham Stencils**™
Blossoms (including hydrangea flowers but not leaves): pp. 37, 41, 46, 47, 56, 60, 62, 63, 67, 74, 90, 91
Carolina Scroll: pp. 44, 54
Clematis: pp. 51, 56, 58, 61, 62, 63, 66, 77, 85
Cottage Window Stencil: pp. 82, 86, 87, 88, 89, 90, 100, 101, 102, 103, 104, 105, 108, 109
Dentil Moulding: pp. 132, 134, 135
English Ivy: pp. 49, 56, 62, 63
Flower Pot: pp. 60, 61
Grapevine: pp. 40, 52, 53
Greek Column: pp. 122, 132, 133
Greek Key Border: pp. 144, 145
Hanging Basket: pp. 56, 62, 63
Honeysuckle Border (not available until January 1998): cover, pp. 44, 54, 55, 68, 69, 80, 130
Hummingbirds: pp. 78, 79
Iris: pp. 64, 65, 66, 74
Iron Work: p. 74
Garden Lattice: pp. 68, 76, 77, 80
Leaf Cluster: pp. 26, 59, 71, 72, 73, 74, 86, 87
Leafy Branch: pp. 37, 59, 67, 71, 74, 91, 126, 127
Mama Cat: pp. 70, 71
Morning Glory with Blossoms Border: pp. 43, 50, 56, 62, 63, 79
Pansy: pp. 48, 60, 61
Picket Fence: pp. 72, 73
Rambling Vine Border: pp. 46, 51, 77, 85
Sword Fern: pp. 23, 73
Terra Cotta Pots: pp. 58, 59, 61
Tulip: pp. 65, 66, 73, 74, 90
Vase: pp. 64, 65
Wisteria: pp. 42, 73, 76, 78, 79

Bibliography

◆ Books on Stencilling

Art of Stencilling, by Lyn Le Grice. Viking, 1986.*

Decorative Stencilling & Stamping, a Practical Guide, by Annie Sloan. Reader's Digest, 1997.*

Stencil It! Kids' Projects, by Sandra L. Buckingham. Camden House, 1993.

Stenciling Techniques, by Jane Gauss. Watson-Guptill Publications, 1995.

Stencilling, a Harrowsmith Guide, by Sandra L. Buckingham. Camden House, 1989.

*contains instructions for spray-paint stencilling

◆ Books on Faux Finishes

Complete Book of Decorative Paint Techniques, by Annie Sloan and Kate Gwynn. Crescent Books, 1994.

Decorative Paint Effects, by Annie Sloan. Reader's Digest, 1996.

Decorative Style, by Kevin McCloud. Simon and Schuster, 1990.

Master Strokes: A Practical Guide to Decorative Paint Techniques, by Jennifer Bennell. Century Hutchinson Australia, 1988.

Paint Magic, by Jocasta Innes. Pantheon, 1981.

Paint Recipes, by Liz Wagstaff. Chronicle Books, 1996.

Paintability, by Jocasta Innes. Weidenfeld & Nicolson, 1986.

Professional Painted Finishes, by Ina Brosseau Marx, Allen Marx and Robert Marx. Watson-Guptill Publications, 1991.

Recipes for Surfaces, by Mindy Drucker and Nancy Rosen. Simon and Schuster, 1995.

◆ Inspirational Books

Decorative Designs, by Graham Rust. Bulfinch Press, 1996.

Grand Illusions: Contemporary Interior Murals, by Caroline Cass. Phaidon Press, 1988.

Painting Murals: Images, Ideas and Techniques, by Patricia Seligman. Macdonald Orbis, 1987.

The Painted House, by Graham Rust. Knopf, 1988.

Trompe l'Oeil at Home: Faux Finishes and Fantasy Settings, by Karen S. Chambers. Raincoast Books, 1991.

Index

Accuracy of natural plant
  forms in freeform projects, 42
Acetate stencils, 14
Acrylic paint, 16
    applying, 16
    applying to canvas, 27
    applying with a roller, 26
    applying with a stencil
      brush, 24
    drying time, 16, 24
    increasing transparency of,
      37
    layering with, 37, 38
    opacity, 16
Acrylic varnish, 16
Adhesive spray, 20; photo, 21
    use, 23
Airbrushes, 18
Applicators, 18
    airbrushes, 18
    rollers, 18
    sponges, 18
    stencil brushes, 18
Artist's brushes, 20; photo, 20
Attic trapdoor skylight,
    project, 81
Backgrounds
    painting, 33
    simplifying, 84
Balusters, stencilling, 70
Balustrades
    and potted palms, project,
      142-143
    stencil patterns, 129, 130,
      143
    stone, project, 130-131
Bed corner hanging, project,
    140-141
Bibliography, 147
Bleeding of paint under stencil,
    23
Blending colors
    in skies, 33
    with solid paint, 25
Borders
    Greek, stencil pattern, 144
    scroll, stencil pattern, 55
    scroll, stencilling, 54
    wall, project, 54-55
Bottles
    liner, photo, 20
    misting, 20; photo, 21
    plastic, 20

shampoo, 20; photo, 21
Boxes, paper, project, 48
Brass stencils, 14; photo, 15
Bridgeless stencilling, 29
Bridgeless stencils, 14
Bridges, 14
Broken color, 28
Brushes, artist's, 20; photo, 20
Brushes, stencil, 18; photos,
    18, 19
    drying thoroughly, 24
    use with acrylic and latex
      paints, 24
Cambric window blind,
    stencilling on, 62
Canvas
    primed, 27
    stencilling on, 27
    unprimed, 27
Card stencils, 14
Carpets. See also Floorcloth
    multicolored, project,
      118-119
    stencilled, 116-119
    tone-on-tone, project,
      116-117
Cat
    by porch railings, project,
      70-71
    stencil pattern, 70
    stencilling, 70
Cellulose sponge, photo, 19
Chez Piggy fence, project, 75
China vase with flowers,
    project, 64-65
Clouds, painting, 33
Cobblestone floor, project, 113
Colors
    adding more than one
      through the same stencil,
      24
    blending solid paint, 25
    broken, 28
    deepening, 24
    mixing, 24
Columns
    stencil pattern, 133
    stone, and dentil border,
      project, 132-133
Commercial stencils, 14
Composition of freeform
    projects, 42-43
Cookie sheets, 20

Crown molding, 132
Curtains, 92-109
    basic stencilling method,
      94-96
    lace, projects, 98-99,
      106-107
    models and sketches, 96
    on windows, 100-109
    on windows, basic method,
      100-101
    tartan on woodgrain door,
      project, 102-103
Curved stencil for draped
    fabrics, 93
Cutter, heat, 20; photo, 20
Cutting mat, 20; photo, 21
Cutting stencils, 22
    opaque, 22
    transparent, 22
    with a heat cutter, 22
    with a knife, 22
Dentil border and columns,
    project, 132-133
Depth, illusion of, 36
Die-cut stencils, 14; photo, 15
Dirt, illusion of, on stencilled
    floors, 115
Doors, 90-91. See also
    Windows
    French, project, 90
    two-sided, project,
      106-109
    veranda, project, 91
    woodgrain, with tartan
      curtain, project,
      102-103
Draped swag, project, 97
Drapery, 92-109. See also
    Curtains
    basic stencilling method,
      94-96
    models and sketches, 96
Easy projects, 46-55, 140-145
Extender, 16
    use, 24
Fabrics, 92-109
    basic stencilling methods,
      60, 94-96
    paints, 16
    patterns, 93
    stencil patterns, 93, 95
Fences, 72-75
    Chez Piggy, project, 75

picket, projects, 72-73
wrought-iron, stencil
    pattern, 75
wrought-iron, stencilling,
    74, 75
Fern leaves, stencil pattern,
    22-23
Fireplace, project, 134-135
Floorcloth, project, 51. See
    also Carpets
Floors, 111-121
    dirt, illusion of, 115
    finishing, 112
    mosaic, project, 120-121
    preparing surface, 112
    stone, projects, 112-113
    terra-cotta tile, project,
      114-115
Flowerpots. See also Planters;
    Pots; Urn
    on shelf, project, 60-61
    stencil patterns, 61
Flowers
    in vases, projects, 64-67
    morning glory, stencil
      pattern, 50
    pansies, stencil patterns,
      48
    stencil patterns, 28, 29,
      32, 41, 46
    wisteria, stencil pattern, 78
Folding screens
    Greek runner on, project,
      144-145
    stone and fabric on,
      project, 130-131
    stone wall and wrought-
      iron fence on, project, 74
Fountain, lion, stencil pattern,
    137
Freeform stencilling, 35-43
    accuracy of plant shapes
      in, 42
    basic method, 36
    composition, 42-43
    layering in, 36, 37-41
    planning, 36, 42, 43
Freehand leaf vines, 31
Freehand shading, 30
Freehand shadows, 30
Freezer-paper stencils, 14;
    photo, 15
French door, project, 90

Fringe, 116
Frisket, liquid, 20; photo, 21
    applicator tool, 41
    how to use, 41
Garden gate, project, 80
Garden wall, project, 136-137
Gingham. See also Plaid
    stencil pattern, 93
    stencilling, 93
Glaze, 16, 24
    shadow, 16
Grape leaves
    mask, 40
    stencil pattern, 52-53
    stencilling, 52
Grapes
    stencil pattern, 52-53
    stencilling, 52
Greek borders, stencil pattern, 144
Greek runner
    on folding screen, project, 144-145
    stencil pattern, 144
Greeting cards, project, 46-47
Hand-cut stencils, photos, 14, 15
Hanging, bed corner, project, 140-141
Hanging basket, project, 62-63
Hard-surface stencilling, 23-26
Head, stone, stencil pattern, 124
Headboard, stencilling, 97
Heat cutter, 20; photo, 20
    use in cutting stencils, 22
Homemade stencils, 14
Honeysuckle
    motif, stencil pattern, 135
    stencil pattern, 55
    stencilling, 54
Hummingbirds, stencil patterns, 78, 79
Hutch, pine, project, 52-53
Hydrangea
    freeform stencilling, 37
    stencil pattern, 41
Idea sources for freeform stencilling, 43
Inside/outside door, project, 106-109
Interference paints, 16
Ivy

stencil pattern, 49
stencilling, 49
Kitchen lattice, project, 77
Knives
    palette, 20; photo, 21
    putty, 20; photo, 21
    use in cutting stencils, 22
    utility, photo, 20
    X-acto, 20; photo, 20
Lace
    curtains, project, 98-99
    using as stencil pattern, 106-107
Lampshade, project, 49
Laser-cut stencils, 14; photo, 15
Latex paint, 16
    applying, 16
    applying to canvas, 27
    applying with a roller, 26
    applying with a stencil brush, 24
    drying time, 16, 24
    increasing transparency of, 37
    layering with, 37, 38
    opacity, 16
Lattice, 76-81
    kitchen, project, 77
    room, project, 78-79
    stencilling, 50
    stencilling, basic technique, 76
Layering, 36, 37-41
    opaque, with latex or acrylic paint, 38
    opaque, with solid stencil paint, 39
    transparent, 37
    with masks, 40-41
    without masks, 37-39
Leaves
    adding veins, 31
    fern, stencil pattern, 22-23
    grape, mask, 40
    grape, stencil pattern, 52-53
    grape, stencilling, 52
    ivy, stencil pattern, 49
    palm, stencil patterns, 104, 142
    stencil patterns, 24, 25, 31, 32, 46

stencilling, 49
    vine. See Vines
Liner bottles, photo, 20
Lion fountain, stencil pattern, 137
Liquid frisket, 20; photo, 21
    how to use, 41
Makeup sponge, photo, 19
Marble fireplace, project, 134-135
Masking fluid, 20. See also Liquid frisket
Masks, 36
    ad hoc, 41
    how to make, 40
    layering with, 40-41
    liquid frisket, 41
    Mylar and paper, 40
    storage, 40
Metallic paints, 16
Misting bottles, 20; photo, 21
Models of drapery and curtains, 96
Molding, crown, 132
Morning glory
    stencil pattern, 50
    stencilling, 50
Mosaic floor, project, 120-121
Mylar
    frosted, proofs, 43
    frosted, stencils, photo, 14
    masks, 40
    stencils, 14; photos, 14, 15
Opaque layering, 38-39
    with latex or acrylic paint, 38
    with solid stencil paint, 39
Opaque stencils, cutting, 22
Overlays, 14, 28-29
Painters' tape, low-tack, 20; photo, 21
    use, 23
Painting materials, sources, 146
Paints, 16
    acrylic, 16
    acrylic, applying, 16
    acrylic, drying time, 16
    acrylic, opacity, 16
    acrylic varnish, 16
    amount to use, 23
    applying to applicator, 23
    applying to canvas, 27
    applying with a roller, 26

    applying with a stencil brush, 24, 25
    bleeding under stencil, 23
    fabric, 16
    interference, 16
    latex, 16
    latex, applying, 16
    latex, drying time, 16
    latex, opacity, 16
    metallic, 16
    solid, 16
    solid, applying with a stencil brush, 25
    solid, blending colors, 25
    solid, drying time, 16
    solid, layering with, 39
    spray, 16
    water-based, 16
    water-based, applying with a brush, 24
    water-based, applying with a roller, 26
Palette knife, 20; photo, 21
Palette tray, 20; photo, 21
Palm
    leaves, stencil patterns, 104, 142
    potted, and balustrade, project, 142-143
Pansies
    stencil patterns, 48
    stencilling, 48
Paper, freezer, stencils, 14
Paper boxes, project, 48
Paper masks, 40
Parrot, stencilling, 104
Pencils
    mechanical, photo, 20
    watercolor, 20; photo, 20
Perspective, 84
Pine hutch, project, 52-53
Place mats, project, 50
Plaid. See also Gingham; Tartan
    stencil pattern, 60
    stencilling, 60
Planning
    alternative plans, 70
    freeform stencilling projects, 36, 42, 43
Plant projects, 57-67
Planters. See also Flowerpots; Pots; Urn

Index

stencil pattern, 58
stencilling, 59
Porch railings, stencilling,
    70-71
Postcards, project, 46-47
Pots. See also Flowerpots;
    Planters; Urn
    stencil pattern, 143
    terra-cotta, stencilling, 59
    topiary trees in, projects,
        58-59
Pouncing, 24
Priming canvas, 27
Projects
    attic trapdoor skylight, 81
    balustrade and potted
        palms, 142-143
    balustrades, stone, 128-131
    basket, hanging, 62-63
    border, columns and
        dentil, 132-133
    borders, wall, 54-55
    carpet, multicolored,
        118-119
    carpet, tone-on-tone,
        116-117
    cat by porch railings, 70-71
    curtain, tartan, on wood-
        grain door, 102-103
    curtains, lace, 98-99
    curtains and drapery,
        92-109
    door, inside/outside,
        106-109
    doors, 90-91, 106-109
    easy, 46-55, 140-145
    fence, Chez Piggy, 75
    fence, picket, 72-73
    fences, wrought-iron, 74, 75
    fireplace, 134-135
    fireplace screen with stone
        urn, 126-127
    floor, cobblestone, 113
    floor, mosaic, 120-121
    floor, paving stones,
        112-113
    floor, rough-cut rock,
        112-113
    floor, terra-cotta tile,
        114-115
    floorcloth, 51
    flowerpots on shelf, 60-61
    gate, garden, 80

greeting cards, 46-47
hanging, bed corner,
    140-141
hanging basket, 62-63
hutch, pine, 52-53
lampshade, 49
lattice, kitchen, 77
lattice room, 78-79
paper boxes, 48
place mats, 50
plants, 57-67
postcards, 46-47
quick, easy and removable,
    140-145
screen, fireplace, with stone
    urn, 126-127
screen, folding, with Greek
    runner, 144-145
screen, folding, with
    wrought-iron fence, 74
swag, draped, 97
terrace, stone, 128-129
trees, topiary, in pots, 58-59
vase, china, with flowers,
    64-65
vases with flowers, 66-67
wall, garden, 136-137
window, four-pane, 86-88
window, leaded, 85
windows, tropical, 104-105
Proofs of stencil components,
    43
Putty knife, 20; photo, 21
Quick projects, 140-145
Railings, porch, stencilling,
    70-71
Reading list, 147
Registration, 14, 28
Removable projects, 140-145
Rock floor, rough-cut, project,
    112-113
Rollers, foam, 18; photo, 18
    loading with paint, 26
    use with acrylic and latex
        paints, 26
Rugs. See Carpets; Floorcloth
Runner, Greek
    on folding screen, project,
        144-145
    stencil pattern, 144
Screens
    fireplace, with stone urn,
        project, 126-127

folding, stencilling on, 74
folding, with Greek runner,
    project, 144-145
Scroll border
    stencil pattern, 55
    stencilling, 54
Sea sponge, photo, 19
Shading, 24, 30
Shadow glaze, 16
Shadows, 30
    on stone, 125
Shampoo bottles, 20; photo, 21
Shelf, with flowerpots, project,
    60-61
Simplifying projects, 84
Sketches of drapery and
    curtains, 96
Sky, painting, 33
Skylight, attic trapdoor,
    project, 81
Solid stencil paint, 16
    applying with a stencil
        brush, 25
    blending colors, 25
    drying time, 16
    layering with, 39
Sources
    of ideas for freeform
        stencilling, 43
    of stencilling materials and
        information, 146-147
Special effects, 30-32
Sponges, 18; photos, 19
Spray adhesive, 20; photo, 21
    use, 23
Spray paints, 16
Squeeze bottles, 20
Stamens, adding, 32
Stems, adding, 32
Stencil brushes, 18; photos,
    18, 19
    drying thoroughly, 24
    use with acrylic and latex
        paints, 24
Stencil card, 14
    stencils, photo, 15
Stencil paint, solid, 16
    applying with a stencil
        brush, 25
    blending colors, 25
    drying time, 16
    layering with, 39
Stencil patterns

balustrades, 129, 130, 143
border, Greek, 144
border, scroll, 55
cat, 70
column, 133
fabrics, 60, 93, 95
fern, 22-23
flowerpots, 61
flowers, 28, 29, 32, 41, 46
gingham, 93
grape leaves, 52-53
grapes, 52-53
honeysuckle motif, 135
honeysuckle vine, 55
hummingbirds, 78, 79
hydrangea, 41
ivy, 49
leaded window, 85
leaves, 24, 25, 31, 32, 46
lion fountain, 137
morning glory, 50
palm leaves, 104, 142
pansies, 48
plaid, 60
planter, 58
pot, 143
runner, Greek, 144
stone head, 124
tartan, 93
tea towel, 94
tile motif, decorative, 114
using real lace as, 106-107
vase, 64
vine leaves, 30
vines, 46
vines, honeysuckle, 55
wisteria, 78
wrought-iron fence, 75
Stencilling
    basic method, 22-29
    freeform, 35-43
    freeform, basic method, 36
    freeform, planning, 36
    materials, sources, 146
    on a hard surface, 23-26
    on canvas, 27
    single stencil, 28
    stress-free, 46
    tools, 18-20
    without bridges, 29
Stencils, photos, 14, 15
    acetate, 14
    brass, 14

card, 14
commercial, 14
cutting, 22
cutting opaque stencils, 22
cutting transparent
    stencils, 22
cutting with a heat cutter,
    22
cutting with a knife, 22
die-cut, 14
freezer-paper, 14
holding in place, 23
homemade, 14
laser-cut, 14
materials and types, 14
Mylar, 14
sources, 146
tin, 14
vinyl, 14
Stippling, 24
Stone, 123-137
    balustrades, project,
        130-131
    basic technique, 124-125
    columns and dentil border,
        project, 132-133
    fireplace, project, 134-135
    floors, cobblestone,
        project, 113
    floors, rough-cut rock,
        project, 112-113
    terrace, project, 128-129
Strathmore Paper Company, 46
Stress-free stencilling, 46
Stretching canvas, 27
Structures, stencilling, 69-81
Swag, draped, project, 97
Swirling, 24
Tape, painters', low-tack, 20;
    photo, 21
    use, 23
Tartan, stencilling, 93. See also
    Plaid
Tea towel, stencilling, 94-95
Tendrils, adding, 32
Terrace, stone, project,
    128-129
Terra-cotta pots, stencilling, 59
Terra-cotta tile floor, project,
    114-115
Three-dimensional appearance,
    30
Ties, 14

Tile floor, terra-cotta, project,
    114-115
Tiles, decorative motif, stencil
    pattern, 114
Tin stencils, 14
Tools, stencilling, 18-20;
    photos, 14-21
        frisket tool, 41
Topiary trees in pots, projects,
    58-59
Towel, tea, stencilling, 94-95
Transparent layers, 37
Transparent stencils, cutting,
    22
Tray, palette, 20; photo, 21
Trees, topiary, in pots, projects,
    58-59
Tropical windows, project,
    104-105
Urn, stone, on fireplace screen,
    projects, 126-127. See also
        Flowerpots; Planters; Pots
Utility knife, photo, 20
Varnish, acrylic, 16
Vases
    china, with flowers,
        project, 64-65
    projects, 64-67
    stencil pattern, 64
Veins, leaf, adding, 31
Veranda door, project, 91
Vines
    honeysuckle, stencil
        pattern, 55
    ivy, stencil pattern, 49
    ivy, stencilling, 49
    leaves, stencil patterns, 30,
        46
    morning glory, stencilling,
        50
    stencilling, 54
Vinyl stencils, 14
Wall, garden, project, 136-137
Wall border, project, 54-55
Water-based paints. See Acrylic
    paint; Latex paint
Watercolor pencils, 20; photo,
    20
Windows, 85-89. See also
    Doors
        four-pane, projects, 86-88
        four-pane, with nonwhite
            frames, 88

larger than four-pane, 88
leaded, project, 85
leaded, stencil pattern, 85
recessed look, 104
tropical, project, 104-105
with curtains, 100-109
with curtains, basic
    method, 100-101
Wisteria, stencil pattern, 78
Woodgrain door with tartan
    curtain, project, 102-103
Wrought-iron fences
    stencil pattern, 75
    stencilling, 74, 75
X-acto knife, 20; photo, 20

Credits

Stencilling

All projects in this book were created and stencilled by the author, with the exception of the following, which were done by Linda Buckingham: place mats, p. 50; topiary, p. 58; curtain, p. 60; lattice room, p. 79; wrought-iron headboard, p. 97.

Prop Loans

Props for many of the photographs in this book were generously loaned by the following sources:

Chintz & Company
901 Homer Street
Vancouver, British Columbia
Canada V6B 2W7

p. 128, freeze-dried topiary, garden pot
p. 132, garden pot
p. 141, tapestry cushion
p. 142, needlepoint cushions

Country Furniture
3097 Granville Street
Vancouver, British Columbia
Canada V6H 3J9

p. 60, wicker basket
p. 103, coat rack, chenille shawl, straw hat
p. 113, wooden stool
p. 121, birdhouses
p. 141, ivory cotton cushions
p. 142, sisal floor covering

Drinkwater and Company
4465 West 10th Avenue
Vancouver, British Columbia
Canada V6R 2H8

pp. 60, 90, wicker basket

OCAY Unpainted Furniture
12542 Bridgeport Road
Richmond, British Columbia
Canada V6V 1J5

p. 53, pine hutch

Peasantries
4429 West 10th Avenue
Vancouver, British Columbia
Canada V6R 2H8

p. 53, napkins, antique iron glass carrier
p. 80, antique painted chair
p. 121, antique German beer-garden chair

Plaza 500 Hotel
500 West 12th Avenue
Vancouver, British Columbia
Canada V5Z 1M2

p. 60, towels

Kanishka Industries
4112 Sunset Boulevard
North Vancouver,
British Columbia
Canada V7R 3Y9

pp. 80, 109, handwoven cotton mats, designed by Rebecca Davies, Vancouver

Upper Crust
4431 West 10th Avenue
Vancouver, British Columbia
Canada V6R 2H8

p. 99, chandelier

Urban Barn
City Square Mall
016-555 West 12th Avenue
Vancouver, British Columbia
Canada V5Z 3X7

p. 75, wrought-iron stand
p. 108, sisal mat
p. 134, wine cooler and stand
p. 140, two foreground cushions

Photography

Clinton Hussey Photography
2-25 East 6th Avenue
Vancouver, British Columbia
Canada V5T 1J3
604-873-1515

Cover photographs; p. 6; p. 8; pp. 44-45; p. 46; p. 47; p. 48; p. 49; p. 50; p. 51; p. 53; p. 54; p. 55; pp. 56-57; p. 58; p. 59 (large photo); p. 60 (large photo); p. 61; p. 63; p. 65; pp. 68-69; p. 71 (large photo); p. 72; p. 73; p. 74 (large photo); p. 75; p. 77; p. 79; p. 80; p. 81; pp. 82-83; p. 85; p. 86 (top two photos); p. 90; p. 91; p. 97; p. 99; p. 100; p. 101; p. 102; p. 103; p. 104; p. 105; p. 108; p. 109; pp. 110-111; p. 113; p. 114; p. 119; p. 121; pp. 122-123; p. 126; p. 128; p. 129; p. 130; p. 131; p. 132; p. 134; p. 135; p. 136; pp. 138-139; p. 141; p. 142; p. 143; p. 145.

Preston Schiedel Photography
574 Princess Street, Suite 204
Kingston, Ontario
Canada K7L 1C9
613-542-7424

pp. 12-13; pp. 14-15; pp. 16-17; pp. 18-19; pp. 20-21; p. 22; p. 24; p. 25; p. 26; p. 27; p. 28; p. 29; p. 30; p. 31; p. 32; p. 33; pp. 34-35; p. 37; p. 38; p. 39; p. 40; p. 41; p. 42; p. 43; p. 59 (small photos); p. 60 (small photos); p. 62; p. 64; p. 71 (small photos); p. 74 (small photos); p. 76; p. 86 (bottom two photos); p. 87; p. 88; p. 94; p. 95; p. 98; p. 106; p. 107; p. 112; p. 115; p. 116; p. 118; p. 120; p. 125.